A HEADLANDS PRESS BOOK

How to Watch a Football Game

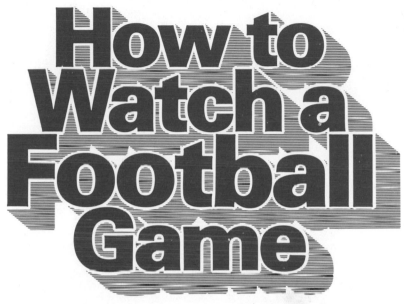

Frank and Lynn Barrett

Diagrams by Robert Evans

Illustrations by Phillip McDonel

AN OWL BOOK

HOLT, RINEHART AND WINSTON
NEW YORK

Copyright © 1980 by Frank and Lynn Barrett and The Headlands Press, Inc.

All rights reserved, including the right to reproduce this book or portions thereof in any form.

Published by Holt, Rinehart and Winston, 383 Madison Avenue, New York, New York 10017.

Library of Congress Cataloging in Publication Data
Barrett, Frank, 1938–
How to watch a football game.
Includes index.
1. Football. I. Barrett, Lynn, joint author.
II. Title.
GV950.6.B37   796.332'02'024
79-3448
ISBN 0-03-056958-3

First Edition
Printed in the United States of America
10 9 8 7 6 5 4 3 2 1

Created and produced by
The Headlands Press, Inc.,
243 Vallejo Street,
San Francisco, California 94111

Project editor
Andrew Fluegelman

Diagram production
Craig DuMonte

Editorial assistance
Linda Gunnarson

Production assistance
Patty King
Susan Sanders
Scott Siedman
Gregory Atwood

Manuscript typing
Willa Crowell

Xerox services
Gregory Hitt

Photographs
Dennis Desprois

Design and production supervision
Howard Jacobsen
Community Type & Design,
Fairfax, California

Composed in Univers 45/75 by
Mimi Moungovan

Mechanical production
Janis Gloystein
Susan Neri
Bob Herbert

Camerawork and
photographic posterization
Sunny Bell

Printing and binding
George Banta Company,
Menasha, Wisconsin

"Hi, Mom!"

Program

The Team

Football is a team effort that combines the commitment and skills of all those associated with the organization. This book was a team effort also. It would not exist without the help of those who gave of their time and shared their knowledge with us.

First, we would like to thank the National Football League coaches who helped us. John Madden, former head coach of the Oakland Raiders, who is now with CBS Sports, read and critiqued the entire manuscript and made many valuable suggestions.

Bill Walsh, formerly assistant coach with the Cincinnati Bengals and San Diego Chargers, former head coach at Stanford University, and presently head coach of the San Francisco 49ers, is largely responsible for our understanding of the intricacies of football strategy. John Ralston, former head coach of the Denver Broncos and now with the 49ers, patiently let us show him the first typeset version of the book; his comments led to revisions of both the text and illustrations. John McVay, former head coach of the New York Giants and currently player personnel director with the 49ers, helped with the strategy section, as did Chuck Studley, the 49ers' defensive coordinator.

We met in Los Angeles with Paul Lanham, formerly special teams coach with the Washington Redskins and Los Angeles Rams and now quarterback coach with the Rams, and it was his insight that crystalized the special teams section of the book. While at the Rams' office, we had the pleasure of meeting with Dan Radakovich, formerly with the Pittsburgh Steelers and now defensive coach of the Rams; in about fifteen minutes he was able to give us a handle on what defensive strategy is all about.

We also had the help of many NFL players and former players. Jim Plunkett, Heisman Trophy winner and Oakland Raider quarterback, helped with the entire project for more than two years.

Y.A Tittle, former quarterback with the 49ers and the New York Giants, gave us his time and suggestions, especially concerning the pros and cons of the quarterback reading the defense.

At the wide receiver position, we had the help of Gene Washington and Billy Wilson, both all-pros formerly with the 49ers. Bruce Taylor, former cornerback with the 49ers, spent an evening with us explaining the subtleties of his position. Dave Morton, middle linebacker with the 49ers, and his brother, Bob, a former football coach, reviewed the manuscript and watched the Super Bowl with us, and their observations and comments appear throughout the book.

We were fortunate to get some insight into Canadian football from Jerry Griffin, who played for seven years as middle linebacker with the Edmonton Eskimos.

We especially want to thank NFL head linesman Burl Toler, who read and critiqued the entire manuscript as well as making suggestions for the Officials, Rules, and Penalties section.

We had help from college coaches too. We attended a clinic at the University of Southern California at which head coach John Robinson spoke about the skill of physical dominance at individual positions, and this became an important part of our strategy section. We also were helped by other USC coaches, especially quarterback coach Paul Hackett and the truly brilliant offensive backfield coach, John Jackson. Gil Haskell, the special teams coach at USC, deserves special thanks. Not only did he read the entire manuscript and help with every phase of the special teams section, but he was also an inspiration for the book itself. We used to hang around and talk football with Gil when he was head coach at St. Ignatius College Preparatory in San Francisco.

Paul Wiggins, head coach at Stanford University, helped with the strategy section. We also had the pleasure of meeting with a truly fine person and legendary college coach, Jim Sochor of the University of California at Davis, who helped us gain an understanding of the philosophy of football.

We owe a very special thanks to Bill Laveroni, former assistant coach at the University of California at Berkeley and currently assistant coach at Utah State University. Bill has been our friend for years, and he, too, was an inspiration for this book. Bill helped us with the project for more than two years, spending countless hours with us, sharing his knowledge of the game. We called on him when we didn't know the answers. Every section of the book reflects his ideas.

We also would like to thank Paul Camera, former Stanford quarterback, for reading and commenting on an early draft of the manuscript. Curt Decker, an NFL timer and college official, also consulted with us.

We were helped by coaches and players from St. Ignatius College Preparatory in San Francisco. Coach Art Beckman worked with us from the beginning, and it was he who finally got us past the jargon of football so that we could understand what other people were saying. Chuck Murphy, also of St. Ignatius, reviewed the entire manuscript and offered many suggestions. Ken Cruz, who was quarterback at St. Ignatius when we started this book and is currently quarterback at City College of San Francisco, also read and commented on the entire manuscript. Other St. Ignatius players who helped us were Brad Chung, Jack Crewe, John Matsuo, and Albert Waters.

We never could have assembled all the information in this book without the generous help of the wonderful people we have mentioned; nevertheless, we take full responsibility for any errors or misstatements that may have found their way into these pages.

There also are many people who worked hard to turn our ideas into a truly remarkable book. Foremost in our appreciation are the talented illustrators who brought this book to life. Robert Evans and Phillip McDonel had to learn what we learned about football before they could even begin to put their extraordinary artistic talents to work. Their dedication to the project went beyond the call of duty. We're also grateful to Dennis Desprois, team photographer for the San Francisco 49ers, whose superb action photos both aided our illustrators and were the basis for the cover and chapter introduction graphics.

The clarity and readability of the book is due to the brilliant design of Howard Jacobsen, who devised the book's deceptively simple format. Underlying each of the diagrams is the careful production work of Craig DuMonte, who diligently turned our scribbles into crisp graphics.

This book never could have come into being had it not been for the support of the people at The Headlands Press, the producer of the book: Barry Traub, who believed in the project all the way, and Linda Gunnarson, who scrutinized every word and helped us to explain things better.

Finally, we want to thank Andrew Fluegelman, president of The Headlands Press and editor of this book. Everything in the book is as much Andrew's as it is ours — that's how closely he worked with us. His name deserves to be on the cover. More importantly, after almost three years of working together, our editor/publisher/author involvement has evolved into one of friendship — the most important relationship that people can have.

Before the Kickoff

Since we've invited you to be our guests and watch a football game with us, we thought we'd introduce our game plan while the teams are warming up down on the field.

■ HOW THIS BOOK CAME TO BE WRITTEN

On December 31, 1977, we were avid, but average, football fans. We watched college games on Saturday, pro games on Sunday, and ate our dinner while watching "Monday Night Football." All that changed the following day, for on New Year's Day, 1978, we began a two-and-a-half-year adventure that was to take us inside football and, finally, to the publication of this book.

It's easy to remember January 1, 1978, because on that day, after watching more than nine hours of football, we realized that we barely knew a fraction of what actually was happening on the field.

We reached that conclusion quite systematically. As we watched the New Year's bowl games, we wrote down in a notebook everything said by the announcers that we didn't understand. By the time the eggnog and turkey had been digested and all the "We're Number Ones" had been proclaimed, we had more than two hundred entries in our notebook, and these didn't even include such expressions as "The cornerback forces," "The defensive end submarined," or "The right offensive guard hooked the defensive tackle," which at the time we took to be merely colorful remarks rather than technical terms that actually explained what these players were doing.

Having collected our initial list of terms, our first step was to go to the library to look for books that, hopefully, would explain to us what this game of football was all about. Well, we found three types of books about football: "My Life Story" books written by famous football players and coaches, picture books with lots of action shots of football games, and technical books about football, written by football coaches for football coaches. Rather than giving us answers, these books only increased the list of terms and questions we'd have to fathom in order to understand what those twenty-two players were up to on each play.

Our next step was presumptuous but rewarding. We sought out football players and coaches and imposed on their patience, graciousness, and generosity to help us come to an understanding of football. We asked a lot of very basic questions, and always received very thorough answers to them. We looked at tapes and films of games and were shown how to spot where the real action was. We even had players demonstrate (on us!) what it's like to be hit by a hook block or a swim rush. Our acknowledgment pages show how many people helped us, but there is no way to fully explain how much they helped us.

In any event, we did come to understand the intricacies of football to the point that, by New Year's Day, 1980, two years after our search began, we were still spectators; but instead of being avid, but average, spectators, we were quite knowledgeable, avid football spectators. We were watching football games differently. We still rooted and booed, but our cheers and jeers were based on understanding. We were still Monday-morning quarterbacks, but our judgment of the Sunday-afternoon quarterback, his teammates, and opponents was tempered by an appreciation of the emotional, physical, and intellectual challenges that football entails. And we were enjoying the game more.

■ WHO THIS BOOK IS FOR

The reason we're telling you all this is because we want you to know that we've written this book for you, the spectators. We've had pro coaches tell us that their players should read it too, and we hope they keep saying it. But this book is really for you, the fan in the stands or in front of the tube.

If you're just becoming interested in football, this book will provide you with the basics for following all the action on the field. On the other hand, even if this is your second, fifth, or fiftieth season as a football fan, we're sure you'll pick up many insights, as well as find clear explanations of techniques, plays, and strategies that may have been puzzling you for years.

We've tried to include all the aspects of football that you're most likely to see in professional games. We've also included and noted special elements of college and high school football. Our comments take into account both what you can see by attending a game and by watching on TV.

■ HOW TO USE THIS BOOK

We're asking you to go along with us for one football game and watch it the way we watch it. We promise that you'll enjoy the game and that when it ends, you're going to have learned more about football than you ever dreamed possible. Here's what we're going to do:

During the First Quarter of the game we'll watch just the offense. We're going to start by learning some basic offensive formations and the names of the positions. Then we're going to watch all the offensive players so we fully understand their jobs. In the Second Quarter we'll follow this procedure for the defense and the special kicking teams. In the Third Quarter we're going to watch the offense and defense interact with the aid of our playbook, and finally, in the Fourth Quarter, we'll sit back and watch the teams implement their strategies. And, whenever we see a referee throw a flag down on the field, we can turn to our

Officials, Rules, and Penalties section so that we know what the striped shirts are looking for.

Our special format for watching the game doesn't mean we don't expect or want you to clap for your favorite team and shake your fist at its opponent, but we bet you'll sit on your hands occasionally instead of doing either, because your appreciation of the skills of all the players will eventually overwhelm you.

Okay, the coin toss is over and the teams are jogging onto the field. Let's watch a football game!

1ST QUARTER

Watching the Offense

During this game, we're not going to try to watch all twenty-two players at once, and we're not going to try to follow the football. Instead, we're going to watch the action as the players and coaches do. We're going to organize our football watching so we can key on certain players or certain moves by each team. By the end of the game, we will feel like we have played every position, executed every play, and considered every strategy decision.

For this first quarter, we're going to watch only the play of the offensive teams; that is, we're going to watch, position by position, whichever team has the football. If possession of the football changes, we'll switch our attention to the other team.

Just because we'll be watching only the offense during this quarter, don't think that we won't see the defense at all. Most of what we'll be watching will focus on what the offense is trying to do to the defense. But for now, stay with us and find out what the offensive game is all about. We'll give equal time to the defense and special teams in the Second Quarter.

Offensive Formations and Positions

We're going to start by looking at four basic offensive formations. This will show us how the offense usually lines up prior to the snap of the ball, and also let us learn the names of the eleven offensive positions. We'll see that the names of some of these positions vary according to the formation.

The one football rule that limits offensive formations states that there must be at least seven offensive players on the line of scrimmage, which is an imaginary line that stretches across the width of the field at the point where the ball is spotted for each play. The rest of the offensive players (other than the quarterback) must be at least a yard behind the line. Aside from this rule, the offensive team can line up in any way. There are, however, a few offensive formations that have proved to be so successful over the years that you are very likely to see them during the game.

■ **THE OPEN SET**
This formation, with seven players on the line of scrimmage, has a basic look to it that you'll see in most offensive formations. This is because another football rule says that only the two players at each end of the line, plus the players in the backfield, are eligible to receive passes. Since a team normally wants to have as many pass receivers as possible, you'll rarely see more than seven players on the line in any formation.

Let's make sure we know the names of the positions in this Open Set formation:

First, there is what is called the 'interior line', whose job is to block. This is made up of the 'center' (C), who is flanked by two 'guards' (LG and RG), who are in turn flanked by two 'tackles' (LT and RT). You can remember the order of this interior line by thinking of them in alphabetical order: center, guard, tackle.

It's important to know these positions because the TV commentators assume you know who and where they are. You can't begin to deal with the notion of a 'pulling guard' or an 'off tackle' play if you don't know the guard from the tackle.

The next player to look at is the 'tight end' (TE). He is on the line of scrimmage next to the five interior linemen, but he's not considered part of the interior line. This is because he is on one end of the line and therefore eligible to catch passes, while the interior linemen are not. But since he might also have to help out and block on running plays, he lines up close, or tight, to the interior line. This is why he is called the tight end.

That seventh player on the left side of the line of scrimmage is an end, too, but he's the 'split end' (SE). He's also eligible to catch passes; in fact, this is his main job. Since he lines up wide of the rest of the line, you'll often hear him referred to as a 'wide receiver'.

Now let's move to the four backfield positions. First, look at the player who is positioned wide to the right flank. He looks like he's on the line, but he's actually a yard behind it. Since he's technically in the backfield, he's a 'back' and is eligible to receive passes. He is called the 'flankerback' or, frequently, simply the 'flanker' (FL). Like the split end, his main job is to receive passes and he is also sometimes called a 'wide receiver'.

There are three backs left. The player who is lined up behind the center is, of course, the 'quarterback' (QB), who receives the ball at the start of each play.

Behind the quarterback are two backs, one behind each tackle, who are called 'running backs', since their main job is to carry and run with the football (although they are also eligible to catch passes). Sometimes you will hear these running backs referred to as the 'fullback' (FB) and 'halfback' (HB). In this formation, the fullback is the running back who is lined up on the same side as the tight end, while the halfback is the running back who is lined up on the other side.

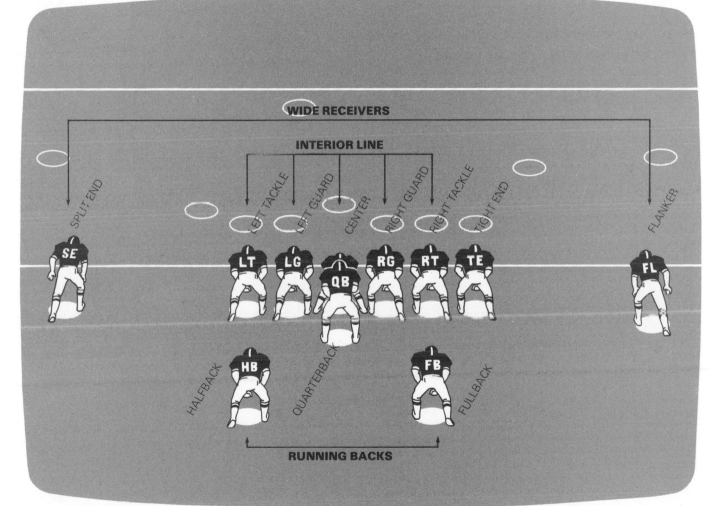

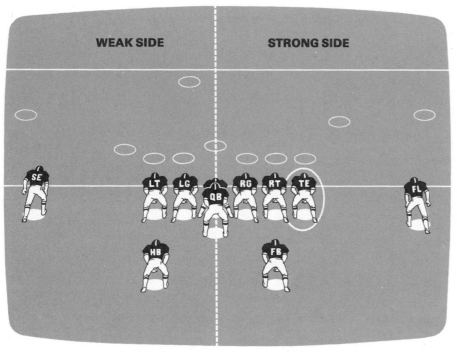

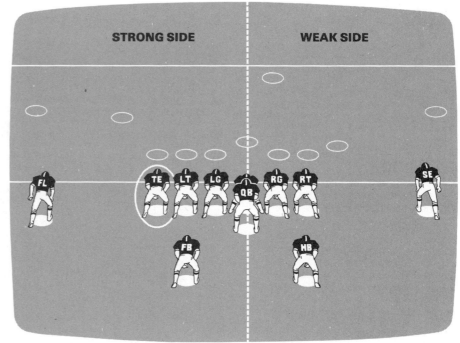

■ STRONG SIDE/WEAK SIDE

Before we look at two variations of the Open Set formation, we'll cover the concept of the 'strong side' and 'weak side'. You'll frequently hear these terms used by the commentators, and they mean very simply: The strong side of the formation is the side on which the tight end lines up; the weak side is the other side of the formation. That's all there is to it. As soon as you know who and where the tight end is you know which is the strong side. The tight end side of the formation is considered 'strong' because there is one more lineman available to block on that side.

The tight end does not have to be lined up on the right side of the line as in our first example. He can also line up on the left. When this happens, the whole formation flip-flops, with the flanker on the left side with the tight end, and the split end on the right. In this case there are three linemen, including the tight end, to the left of the center, and so the tight end strengthens the left side of the formation for running plays.

For consistency's sake, we are going to show the tight end on the right side of the formation in all of the diagrams in this book, so the strong side will always be on the right side in our examples. But you should remember that the tight end can line up on either side.

When you hear a TV commentator talk about the 'strong side guard' or about a 'running play to the strong side', this means the side where the tight end lines up. And when you hear about the 'weak side tackle' or about a 'pass to the weak side', this refers to the side of the field where there is no tight end.

Later, we'll see that even the defensive positions are often referred to by this strong and weak side terminology, but we'll wait until the Second Quarter to look at the defense.

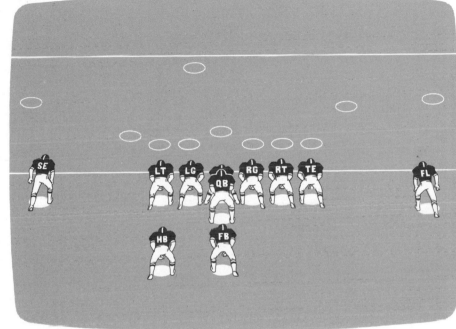

■ STRONG SIDE SET

There are two variations of the Open Set that you'll see frequently. In the Strong Side Set, one running back, the fullback, is lined up behind the quarterback while the other, the halfback, is on the tight end side of the line (the strong side), behind his tackle. This formation is also called the 'Near Side Set', which means the halfback is lined up near the tight end. Notice that except for the two running backs all the other players are lined up exactly as they were in the Open Set and that the names of these positions remain the same.

■ WEAK SIDE SET

Here the fullback is once again the running back behind the quarterback, but the halfback is on the weak side (opposite side from the tight end), behind his tackle.

This formation also goes by the name 'Far Side Set'. This means that the halfback is lined up far from the tight end rather than near him as he was in the Strong Side Set. Notice again that all that has changed in this formation are the positions of the two running backs. The other nine players are positioned as they were in the previous formations.

The Interior Line

Now we'll watch some action on the football field. The area where the five members of the interior line do battle is often called the 'trenches' or the 'pits'. Since it's a well-known football axiom that "the game is won in the trenches," it's only natural that we start by watching the offensive interior line.

The interior line is made up of the biggest and heaviest players on the offense. Their forte is not speed, but brute strength combined with agility. As we'll see, their job demands just these push-and-shove physical abilities. On running plays, the interior line has to make space, or open holes, for the ball carrier to go through. On passing plays, its main job is to protect the quarterback so he has time to find his receivers and throw a pass.

■ THE I FORMATION

The I Formation is another basic offensive formation. The only difference between it and the previous formations is again the alignment of the two running backs. In the I Formation, the running backs line up in a straight line, or letter 'I', behind the quarterback.

The back who is directly behind the quarterback is called the 'fullback', while the back lined up behind him at the tail of the formation is called the 'tailback'. The names of all the other positions in this formation are the same as in the previous formations.

These are four of the formations that you're most likely to see in a pro or college game. At the end of this quarter we'll take a look at some other offensive formations.

■ THE CENTER

Most of the time we're going to watch the interior line as a unit, but first we'll watch each of the interior line positions. Notice that the center lines up slightly ahead of the guards and tackles. This is because he has to hold the football and 'snap', or 'hike', it to the quarterback. All the other players must stay behind the tip of the football until the ball has been snapped. If any player other than the center violates this neutral zone prior to the snap of the ball, his team is penalized for being offside.

The center is, in effect, the field general for the interior line. We'll soon see that each lineman has a blocking assignment on each play. It's the center's job to call out adjustments to these assignments just before the start of the play, if he feels such adjustments are necessary because of what he sees defensively.

■ SNAPPING THE BALL

If you watch closely, you might be able to see that as the center takes his position he holds the ball so that the laces are to his left (if his quarterback is right-handed). At the quarterback's signal, the center snaps the ball through his legs in a quarter-turning motion so that the football ends up parallel to the line of scrimmage, with the fingers of the quarterback's passing hand across the laces of the ball.

Unlike the other offensive linemen, the center must do two things at once. He has to snap the ball back through his legs to the quarterback and at the same time move forward or backward to block the defense. If he waited to move until after he had snapped the football he would be giving up the advantage he has of knowing the precise instant the play will begin, and that could be the difference between remaining upright and ending up on the ground.

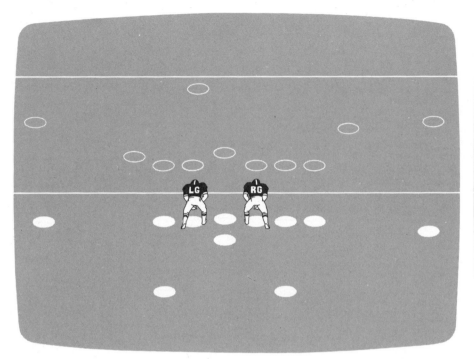

■ THE GUARDS

Now look at the men to the left and right of the center. The guards are lined up a bit behind the center in a 'three-point' stance; that is, with one hand on the ground. On normal plays they are split about three feet to the left and right of the center. When very short yardage is needed they will tighten up this split and move closer to the center.

The guards will have to move forward to block for the ball carrier or back to protect the passer at the instant the ball is snapped, but not before, or they will be penalized for being offside. We'll soon see that guards must also be able to 'pull out' and back from their positions in the line, run to the right or left, and then 'cut back' into the line to block for a running play to the right or left.

■ THE TACKLES

The job of the tackles is the same as the guards: blocking on running plays and pass protection for the quarterback on passing plays. The tackles also block forward or back when the ball is snapped, but, unlike the guards, they are rarely called on to pull out of the line to block and open holes elsewhere in the line.

The tackles are often the strongest and heaviest players on the offense. It is the strength of the tackles that leads many teams to favor the 'off tackle' play, as they rely on the tackles to open holes at their positions.

Interior Line Patterns

Let's expand our vision and watch the members of the interior line do their job as a unit. These interior line patterns are the same offensive activity that the defense 'reads' or 'keys' to know what the offense is up to, and they want to know this even more than we do.

Occasionally, the interior line will be moving contrary to the following patterns just to confuse the defense, but you'll be surprised how often these basic patterns are a reliable key to the play.

■ LINE MOVES FORWARD

If you see the center, guards, and tackles move forward at the snap of the ball, they're very likely trying to open up a running hole through the center of the defensive line. You can expect a ball carrier to come crashing through somewhere just behind them. This forward movement of the interior line is a reliable clue that the play is an 'inside' running play, which is any running play that goes between the two offensive tackles.

■ MAN BLOCKING

The simplest blocking scheme with the line moving forward is 'man' blocking, used mainly on straight ahead running plays. In our example, each interior lineman blocks the defensive man directly in front of him. The ball carrier follows this surge, picks out the biggest hole, and plows forward. An alternative to this simple scheme is 'zone' blocking, in which each lineman is assigned to block an area rather than a specific man.

■ LINE MOVES SIDEWAYS

If the line moves in a slanting or sweeping direction to either side, this is a tip-off that the play is probably a running play to that side. If the interior line unit appears to move right it is likely that it will be a running play to the right. If the interior line unit moves left it is probably going to be a running play to the left. (Sometimes one lineman may 'block back' in the opposite direction from the general flow.)

■ PULLING AND CUTTING

In our example, you can see a typical blocking scheme when the line moves sideways. Both the right and left guards have 'pulled' out of the line, run to the left, and then 'cut' back into the area that is to be opened for the ball carrier. This pulling and cutting by the guards is an essential interior line technique on 'outside' plays (outside the offensive tackles) that can often open the door for a spectacular running play.

■ LINE RETREATS

If the interior line unit does not move forward or to either side, you and the defense can react to a probable passing play. On a passing play the interior linemen will stand and back-pedal to form a protective pocket for the quarterback to give him as much time as possible to find his passing target and throw the football. Any time you see the interior linemen come out of their stance and stand up, think "pass."

■ PASS DROP

Our example shows a typical 'pass drop' by the interior line. Balance is very important to these players who are forming the pocket; their knees are bent, and they try to maintain control by staying directly in front of the defenders rushing the quarterback.

Interior Line Blocking

The offensive linemen don't just randomly bang away at their opponents to get their job done. They choose from a number of specific blocking techniques designed to produce specific results.

Offensive players are allowed to use their hands and arms to block, but they can't use them to grab or encircle their opponents. To be completely truthful, the outstanding offensive players do learn to use their hands and hold from time to time without being caught by the officials, and this is more or less accepted as part of the art of blocking.

These blocks are important. Take turns watching all five of the interior linemen use these blocking techniques.

■ DRIVE BLOCK

This is the bread-and-butter block of the offensive linemen. It is used to 'drive' a defensive lineman back off the line of scrimmage when that defensive man is lined up straight in front of the offensive lineman. The goal of this block is to move a defensive man back and out of the way so a hole can be opened for the ball carrier. Notice that the interior lineman aims his block directly at the numbers of the defensive player.

■ SHOULDER BLOCK

Here's the block that is used if the defensive lineman is lined up to the side, so that a straight ahead drive block is not possible, or if the offensive lineman's assignment is to move the defender to one side. The offensive lineman comes out of his stance and then drives his shoulder into the defender's inside number. Also notice that the offensive lineman keeps his elbow and forearm high so he has an extra wide blocking surface.

■ HOOK BLOCK

This block is used by the interior lineman to keep a defender from making penetration toward the outside. On the 'hook' block the offensive lineman comes out of his stance and then turns sideways to contain the defender. This block is also called the 'reach' block since the offensive lineman reaches around his defensive opponent's outside shoulder.

■ SCRAMBLE BLOCK

Sometimes the offensive lineman doesn't want to move his defender back or to the right or left, but just wants to stop him from moving forward toward the play. Or sometimes the defender may be too far away for a drive or shoulder block to be used effectively. In these situations you may see a 'scramble' block. The offensive lineman throws himself on all fours in front of the defender's knees to trip him up and take him out of the play. This block is also called the 'cut-off' block.

■ PASS BLOCK

On a passing play, the offensive line wants to give the quarterback as much time as possible to find a receiver and pass the ball. Watch how the offensive linemen execute 'pass' blocks by rising from their stance, stepping backward, and then slamming their fists against the chests of the rushing defensive men. In college and high school football the offense is not allowed to use fists on this block.

The assignment of the offensive linemen on passing plays is to keep their bodies between the quarterback and the pass rushers, and you'll see them trying to do this at all costs.

Blocking Schemes

When we watched the interior line move as a unit, we saw three of the most basic blocking schemes: man blocking, pulling and cutting, and the pass drop. Now we're going to look at some alternate schemes that are used to try and fool the defense. Teamwork is essential in all these blocking schemes, which are practiced repeatedly by the interior line. Virtually all the activity we are watching is planned and decided before the play begins—not made up on the spot.

■ CROSS

This scheme attempts to fake out the defense by exchanging man assignments rather than blocking straight ahead. In our example, the left guard crosses to block the man on his left, while the left tackle crosses just behind the guard to take on the defender to his right. In addition to the element of surprise, this scheme provides the offensive linemen with better blocking angles against certain types of defensive rushes.

■ FOLD

The fold block is similar to the cross, but it involves the second man taking a step backward and then blocking to the side. In our example, the right tackle crosses to his left, while the right guard 'folds' back to take on his man parallel to the line. On an actual play, each of these schemes would be designed to open or protect a specific area for the ball carrier, or when the defense is expected to rush from a certain angle.

■ TRAP BLOCK

In this scheme, an offensive lineman steps out of his position and moves across the line to hit a defender from the side. Our example shows the left guard pulling and 'trap' blocking to the right side of the line. Frequently, in order for this scheme to work, the defender must be distracted so that he is unaware that a trap block is coming his way.

■ INFLUENCE BLOCK

The 'influence', or 'sucker', block is not really a block, but a fake by an offensive lineman to fool or distract a defender. In our example, the right tackle steps back as if to pass block. The influence block is often used to lure a defender into a trap block.

■ CO-OP BLOCK

This scheme is used to try and get a momentary 'two-for-one' advantage over one defender. In our example, the center has first moved over to his left, to help out the left guard with his block. Once the guard's man has been slowed down with the center's help, the center spins and continues forward to block another defender.

This is different from a 'double-team' block, in which two linemen block one man. We'll look at this block later when we watch the tight end position.

The Running Backs

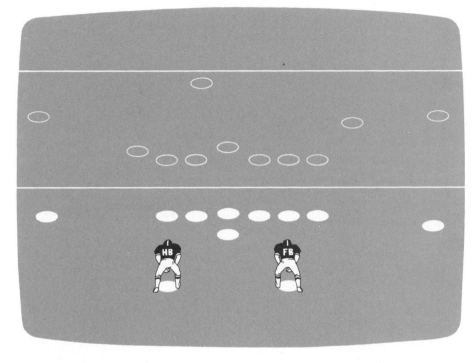

We're going to turn our attention now to the two running backs. There are really two types of running backs. One running back, the fullback, is usually recruited for running and blocking strength that will enable him to lead interference and block for the ball carrier, or bull his way forward with the ball on short yardage running plays. The other type of running back, the halfback, is usually recruited for running speed that will allow him to streak through holes opened by the offensive line, or to get outside and around the defense.

We're also going to start considering which types of plays are likely to result from different formations. These 'predictions' are based on actual game probabilities, but keep in mind that football is a game of trickery. Some of the most spectacular plays often result from doing the unexpected.

■ THE FULLBACK AND HALFBACK (OPEN SET)

Before we start watching the many jobs of the two running backs, let's make sure we can pick them out prior to the start of the play. They will usually be lined up in back of the quarterback. In the Open Set they are split, with the fullback behind the tackle on the tight end side and the halfback behind the tackle on the weak side. This is frequently a passing formation. You are likely to see the running backs either go out to run a pass pattern or stay in the backfield and block to protect the quarterback.

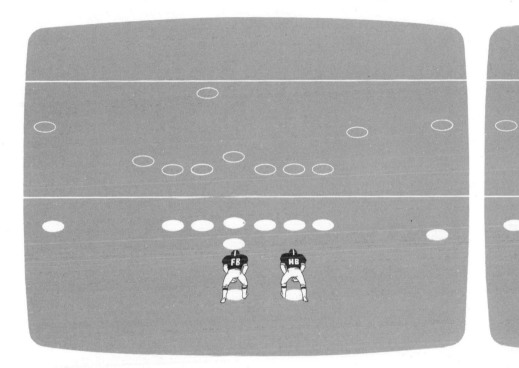

■ THE FULLBACK AND HALFBACK (STRONG AND WEAK SIDE SETS)

Our example shows the Strong Side Set. The fullback is lined up behind the quarterback and the halfback is lined up behind the tackle on the strong, or tight end, side. If our example were the Weak Side Set, the halfback would line up behind the tackle on the left, or weak, side. Both these formations favor running plays.

■ THE FULLBACK AND TAILBACK (I FORMATION)

In the I Formation, the back closest to the quarterback is the fullback. The back behind him, at the tail of the formation, is called the 'tailback'. This is usually a running play formation.

Frequently you'll see the running backs shift from one formation into another one before the start of the play. They do this to confuse the defense, and we'll watch this in more detail later.

Ball Handling

Now we're going to watch the running backs carry the football. This covers a lot of different activities. When a running back receives the football directly from the quarterback, it is called a 'handoff'. A running back also has to be able to fake as if he has received a handoff. The quarterback may also toss the ball to the running back by using a 'pitchout', or 'lateral'.

Once the running back has the ball, he has to be able to tuck it away and carry it properly.

■ THE HANDOFF

The running back who gets the handoff will be running at full speed toward the line when he receives the ball from the quarterback. The quarterback places the ball on the running back's belt buckle. Once the running back feels the ball on his stomach, he closes his elbow and cradles the ball with both arms. He doesn't look down, as he needs to focus all his energy and attention on his point of attack through the line of scrimmage.

■ THE FAKE HANDOFF

On the fake handoff, the faking running back may have the ball for only a split second, or not at all. As the quarterback places his hand or the ball on the running back's stomach, the running back clamps his arms and pretends he is carrying the ball, going in a different direction from the real ball carrier. The fake handoff can be as effective as blocking a man, as usually at least one defender will follow the faking running back.

■ RECEIVING THE PITCH-OUT

If a play is going to be run to the outside of the offensive tackles, the quarterback may toss the ball to the running back instead of handing it off. This 'lateral', or 'pitch-out', allows the running back to build up speed and get to his point of attack quicker than if the quarterback used a handoff.

You will see this exchange accomplished in two different ways. On the 'shovel pass', the quarterback takes the snap from the center, turns, and spirals the ball underhand to the running back. Or, the quarterback might turn and 'dead ball' a floating underhand pass to the running back. The spiral gets there faster but the dead ball is easier to catch.

The running back who receives the pitch-out will have the palm of one hand up and the palm of the other hand down so he can take in the ball, and, most important, he'll watch the ball into his hands until he is sure he has caught it.

■ CARRYING THE FOOTBALL

Carrying the football correctly is often the difference between gaining yardage and a fumble, and fumbles are a disaster. One point of the football should rest in the palm of the running back's hand while the opposite point of the football is tucked into his armpit. The points of the football should never be exposed. If you see a running back carrying the football in one hand like a loaf of bread, you can bet he's a fumble-prone running back.

Once the running back owns the football, he must protect it at all costs. The ball carrier will usually try to carry the football on the side away from where he is likely to be tackled, and for this reason you'll often see a running back switch the ball from one arm to the other when he is running with the football.

Blocking and Running

Once one of the running backs has the football, the open field blocking and running skills of the running backs come into play. Usually, one running back will be carrying the ball and the other running back will be leading interference and blocking for him. Both jobs are essential to the success of the play. The ball carrier can't depend on gaining much yardage unless his other running back helps him. Great blocking makes great running backs.

Incidentally, running with the football is also called 'rushing'. When you hear that a certain player holds the record for rushing, this does not refer to his racing through airports, but to the long chunks of yardage he has gained while carrying the football.

■ LEAD BLOCKING

The running back without the football usually leads open field blocking interference for his teammate who carries the ball. This 'lead' blocker must follow the route called for by the play and block out any converging defender.

The running backs use basically the same blocks that we saw the interior line use a few plays ago, the main difference being that the backs are running at their opponents.

■ FOLLOWING BLOCKERS

The running back with the ball will follow his blockers, unless the play calls for him to do otherwise. Of course, if the blocking breaks down or fails to materialize, the running back will try to get the job done on his own, but his job is always easier (and less painful) if he can follow the blocking that is being set up for him.

■ STRAIGHT ARM

Most running backs try to keep their shoulder pads lower than the defensive man trying to make a tackle because, by keeping low, there is less target for the tackler to hit.

One way to ward off tackles is the 'straight arm'. When the ball carrier sees a defender about to make a tackle, he thrusts his arm straight at the defender with his elbow locked and pushes the tackler away with his outstretched palm. The running back uses the straight arm only at the last second. If he put his arm out too early, the defensive man might tackle him by grabbing his arm.

If the running back knows he is about to be tackled, the safest move is for him to cover and protect the ball with his free hand.

■ SPIN-OUT

Another technique for avoiding tackles is the 'spin-out'. If the running back with the ball runs into a defensive player, he'll suddenly change his direction with a twisting move in an attempt to break out of the grasp of the tackler.

As you watch the running backs, you'll see varying rushing styles, all designed to avoid tackles. Some backs are agile and fleet-footed, and use these abilities to outrun or outmaneuver the defenders. Other backs rely more on their ability to break out of tackles with moves like the straight arm and spin-out. Finally, some running backs simply rely on their power, and are known for being able to drag two or more tacklers with them for an extra five yards on each play.

Running Patterns

Now we're going to watch the running back who carries the football and focus our attention on *where* he goes as he is carrying the ball.

All running plays are designed to go through one of ten imaginary holes, or running lanes, that are spaced across the width of the football field. The running hole that is attacked will, of course, depend on the play that has been called in the huddle. It's easy to see these holes open up during the play when the TV camera shows the play as if you were watching from the end zone. This is why many coaches and scouts prefer to view the game from this perspective.

The following are basic running patterns which are easy to spot. Later, in the Third Quarter, we'll look at our playbook to see the individual assignments of each of the offensive and defensive players on these plays.

■ RECOVERING FUMBLES

As long as we're watching the ball carrier, we should say a bit about recovering fumbles. Once the ball has been fumbled (dropped by a ball carrier during a play), it's anyone's football. The man who recovers it, either offense or defense, owns it for his team. When a defensive player recovers a fumble (or intercepts a pass), this is called a 'turnover'. A turnover can be the break that means winning or losing the game.

Everyone will try to recover the fumble, especially the player who was unfortunate enough to drop the ball. Although in professional ball it is legal to pick up a fumble and run, the safest way to recover a fumble is to jump on top of the ball and hang onto it with arms, legs, and stomach.

■ RUNNING HOLES

All running plays are aimed to attack areas, gaps, or potential running holes across the football field. Our diagram shows these holes according to a 'gap' numbering system used by many teams. The gaps between the offensive players on the right side are numbered with even numbers, starting with zero; the gaps on the left side are given odd numbers.

Holes zero through three are inside the two offensive tackles. These are the areas where 'inside' plays are run. Hole number four is between the right tackle and tight end, while hole five covers the area between the left tackle and where the tight end is when he plays on the left side. These are the 'off tackle' areas. Holes six through nine are outside the tight end position on each side. These are the areas where 'outside' plays are run.

Some teams use numbering systems that put the holes 'over' the offensive players, rather than between them, but every team has some way to identify these running areas.

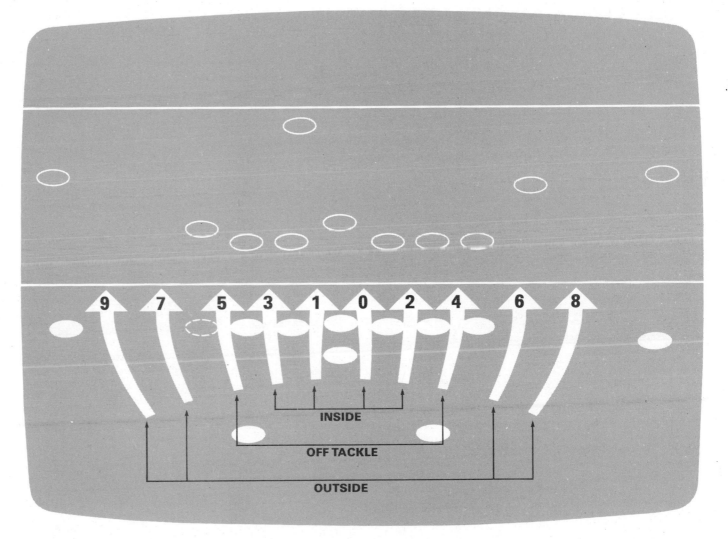

■ DIVE

The 'dive', or 'line buck', is a favorite charge of a ball carrier when his assignment calls for him to ram the line for short yardage, through one of the holes between the two tackles. On the dive pattern the ball carrier is on his own; the other running back does not lead interference. You will see this used when the offense is within feet of a first down or close to the opponent's goal line.

The running back will take the football and tuck it into his stomach, cradling it with both arms. He will keep his body low and his head up and erupt through the line behind his blockers on the offensive line. In a goal line situation, the running back will often try to vault up and over his blockers.

The line buck is the strong suit of some running backs, who are often brought into the game just for the purpose of picking up short yardage.

■ BLAST

The direction of the 'blast' is also the inside area between the two tackles, but on this pattern, one running back leads interference while the running back who gets the handoff follows him. This is a quick opener, used primarily for short yardage; however, with good blocking, a fleet runner, and extra effort, the running back may break loose for a big gain.

During this pattern, the running back should have both hands and arms wrapped around the ball, as it could easily be knocked loose as he plows through the army of defenders.

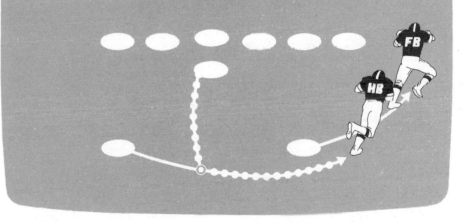

■ OFF TACKLE

An 'off tackle' run is a quick diagonal run, usually through the area occupied by the strong side tackle who is lined up next to the tight end. Since the running back must run a longer distance to get to the off tackle hole, this pattern takes longer to develop than the blast or dive. Consequently the running back is usually led and blocked for both by the other running back and by one or both pulling guards. The reason this pattern is popular and often successful is because the strongest players on the offensive interior line are usually the two tackles and because the strong side tackle will often get help in the form of a two-man, or 'double-team', block from his tight end.

The off tackle run can also be to the weak side, but in this case there is no tight end and so no double-team block advantage.

■ SWEEP

You will know you are seeing a 'sweep' pattern develop when the running back with the football circles out of the backfield and runs toward one of the outside holes near the sideline. As you watch, you'll realize that there is an advantage and a disadvantage to this pattern. The advantage is that the running back gets to run a long way, gaining speed and momentum, and has time to pick up blocking help from his teammates as the guards pull out of the line and lead the blocking. This pattern also attacks an area of the field where only a few defensive men are lined up at the start of the play.

On the negative side, however, the running back has to run a long way before he can gain yardage by 'turning the corner' and heading downfield. Coaches stress that the running backs must make this turn quickly, or, as they say, "Go north and south and not east and west."

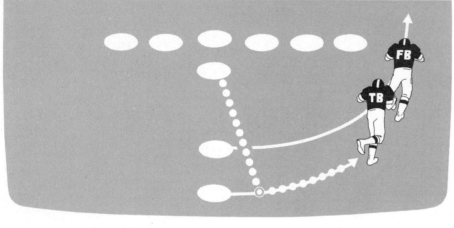

■ PITCH

The pitch-out is a method of getting the ball to a running back, but you'll also hear commentators refer to the offense running a 'pitch' pattern. On the pitch, the ball is lateralled to the running back. The pattern is faster developing than one using a handoff, since the running back receives the ball on a run while headed for his running hole.

A pitch can be used on an off tackle pattern, but usually it signals a sweep to the outside.

■ COUNTER

The 'counter' is one of a number of 'misdirection' patterns in which the ball carrier goes in an opposite direction from the flow of the play. In this illustration, the fullback fakes a lead block to the left side while the halfback runs in a counter-direction to the right side of the line. This pattern must be coordinated with the offensive line blocking. We'll look at both in more detail in the Third Quarter when we look at plays.

■ CUTBACK

The 'cutback' is a misdirection pattern in which the ball carrier starts to follow his lead blocker, but then cuts back against the flow of the play. In this illustration, the fullback is lead blocking to the right side. The tailback, carrying the ball, starts his run to the right, then cuts through the left side of the line. This type of pattern demands a talented back good at open field running without lead blocking.

■ REVERSE

There are several variations on the 'reverse' pattern, but all involve a ball carrier heading in one direction, then handing off to another player, who carries the ball in the opposite direction. In this illustration the halfback receives the handoff from the quarterback, sweeps right, then hands off to the flanker, who carries the ball around to the left.

This is a trick misdirection pattern that involves several risks. First, it takes a long time to develop; the ball stays in the backfield for some time before the final ball carrier can turn the corner and head downfield. Also, the double handoff increases the chance of a fumble. For these reasons, the reverse pattern is a gamble that might lead to a spectacular running gain, but could also result in a loss, or even a turnover.

Running Back Pass Routes

Running backs are also called upon to run pass routes. Often these routes are designed to give the quarterback an outlet, or 'safety valve', man to throw to if the other pass receivers are covered. Running backs also run pass routes to ease the pressure on the quarterback; if a running back runs a pass pattern, a defensive player usually has to cover him rather than rush the quarterback. When a running back forces a defender to cover him, this also can ease the pressure on other pass receivers. Such a move is called running a 'clearing route'.

We'll take a look now at some of the pass routes frequently run by the running backs. Then we'll look at some more pass routes, and pass catching techniques, when we watch the wide receivers.

■ FLARE

On the 'flare', or 'swing', route the running back takes off in a horizontal direction for the nearest sideline, as the halfback is doing in our example. If the quarterback is about to be tackled and can't spot a receiver downfield, he can dump off a pass to the running back, who can take it and charge forward for yardage. We will see later that the flare pattern is also used to set up the screen pass play.

■ SHOOT

When a running back runs a 'shoot' route he heads straight downfield through one of the areas between the tackles and wide receivers, as illustrated here by the fullback. This is about a five-yard route; when this distance is reached the running back will turn quickly and look for the pass.

This is sometimes called a 'seam' route because it heads for a seam between the pass defense zones (which we'll look at later).

■ FLAT

Later we will see that the 'flat' zone is one of the 'underneath', or 'short', zones protected by the defense on pass plays. There are two flat zones, one on each side of the field, and a flat pass route is a quick angular run to either of these two zones, as illustrated here by the halfback.

■ CURL

Later we will see that the 'curl' zones are underneath, or short, zones in the middle of the field, next to the two outside flat zones. The curl routes are short routes that loop into these zones, as shown here by the fullback.

■ PASS BLOCK

Running backs are sometimes assigned the job of staying back rather than running pass routes so that the quarterback has extra protection and, consequently, more time to locate a receiver and get off an accurate pass. When the running back stays back, as the halfback is doing here, he must be able to pass block and help form the protective pocket that circles the quarterback.

■ SAFETY VALVE

Many of the pass routes run by the running backs are 'safety valve' routes, in that they are designed to provide the quarterback with a safe man to throw the ball to if the quarterback is in danger of being tackled. Even if the running back stays back to pass block, he will still stay available to offer the quarterback a last-second outlet, as the fullback is doing in the illustration.

The Wide Receivers

The passing game, or 'air game', is an essential weapon of a successful offensive attack, and the two stars of this offensive passing game are the lightning speedster wide receivers. Some professional wide receivers can run forty yards in 4.3 to 4.4 seconds and a hundred yards in about 9.2 seconds. This is extremely fast. The wide receivers are expected to be in position to catch passes at all spots on the field, but they seem to get most of their attention for their ability to get down the field quickly and catch the long pass, or 'bomb'.

We'll see that speed is not the wide receivers' only weapon, however. They must be able to fake out their defensive opponents so that they are open to catch passes, and they even play roles on running plays.

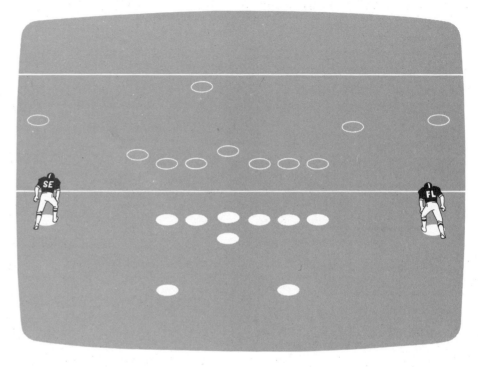

■ THE SPLIT END

Let's review the terminology that is used to describe the wide receiver positions. Notice that one wide receiver plays on the line of scrimmage, but is split way off to the side. He's called the 'split end'.

■ THE FLANKER

The wide receiver who is flanked to the strong side, about a yard behind the line of scrimmage, is known as the 'flankerback', or simply the 'flanker'. As we mentioned earlier, the flanker plays behind the line so that the tight end will also be eligible to receive passes. Aside from this fact, there is no practical difference between the roles of the flanker and split end, and you'll frequently hear them both called simply the 'wide receivers'.

Wide Receiver Moves

We'll soon see that the wide receivers have pass routes that get them to certain spots on the field, in position to catch passes. From the moment the wide receivers take off on these pass routes, they will be dogged by the pass defenders, whose job it is to make sure they don't come up with a reception. To combat this defense, the wide receivers have a number of moves which they use to try and foil the defenders.

■ STANCE AND RELEASE

Some wide receivers get down in a 'four-point' stance, with both hands on the ground, much like a starter in the 100-yard dash. Most, however, stand upright. The down stance allows the wide receiver to take off quickly, but the upright stance lets the wide receiver monitor the pass defense from the instant the play begins. Since he is too far away to hear the quarterback calling his signals, the wide receiver watches for the snap of the ball.

Once the ball is snapped, the wide receiver pushes off his back foot and starts the beginning, or 'stem', of his pass route. The timing of this 'release' is important if the receiver is to get a good jump on the play and into his route. He'll either run directly at his defensive opponent or to the defender's inside or outside.

■ MOVE AND BREAK

The wide receiver's 'move' occurs just before he is about to commit himself to his pass route. When the wide receiver reaches this spot he tries to trick the defender by faking with his head, hips, or feet so the defender will think he's going one way when he's really going another.

After the wide receiver has put his move on the defender he'll 'break' toward the spot where he's supposed to end up on his assigned pass route, hoping that he can shake loose his defender. If all goes well, the pass will be there to greet him.

■ CRACKBACK BLOCK

When a wide receiver is called upon to block on a running play he is usually assigned a man to block within five yards of the line of scrimmage, in what is called a 'crackback' block. This block is usually a surprise to the defender, as his attention is focused on the offensive line.

A crackback block is legal so long as it doesn't hit the opponent from behind or below the waist. An illegal crackback block subjects the offensive team to a penalty. A wide receiver who crackback blocks is no longer eligible to receive a pass on the play.

Wide Receiver Pass Routes

If you are at the game in person, it is great fun watching the intricate pass routes run by the wide receivers on virtually every play. Unfortunately, if you're watching the game on TV, it is not as easy to follow the pass routes of the wide receivers, who quickly disappear downfield while the TV focuses its attention on the line of scrimmage and the quarterback. This is surprising, since sometimes it is obvious that a play will be a pass, and it would be far more interesting to see a larger area of the field so we could follow these pass routes and the defensive pass coverage.

The instant replay sometimes shows us the wide receiver to whom the ball was thrown, but even then the tendency is for the replay to show us the pass and the catch rather than the pass route. Until we get a more complete TV view, at least we can have a clear mental picture of these routes so we can understand what's happening out of view of the camera.

■ SLANT

On a 'slant' route, the wide receiver will run out from his position in a slanting angle to the spot where the pass will be thrown, as illustrated here by the split end. The most hazardous slant route is across the middle, as the wide receiver can be belted by a number of defenders after he catches the football.

■ FLY

The 'fly', or 'streak', pass route is run straight downfield from the wide receiver positions, illustrated here by the flanker. This is designed to get the wide receiver free for a long pass, and has a lot in common with the old schoolyard play of "Everyone out for a long one." This is also called a 'go' or 'bomb' route.

■ POST

On the 'post' route, the wide receiver runs toward the center of the field in the area of the goal posts. This is a pass route for long yardage, or, hopefully, a touchdown.

■ FLAG

This is called the 'flag' route because there used to be flags at the corners of the end zone and the wide receivers would run downfield, aiming their routes at these flags. Now this is often referred to as a 'corner' route. This is also a long pass route which you will see run when the quarterback is planning to throw a 'bomb'.

■ SQUARE-IN

On the 'square-in', or 'down-and-in' route, the wide receiver runs downfield and then cuts toward the center of the field for the pass. The square-in route is a bit dangerous, as it leaves the wide receiver open to be nailed by one or more defensive players.

■ SQUARE-OUT

On the 'square-out', or 'down-and-out' route, the wide receiver runs straight downfield and then cuts at a ninety-degree angle toward the nearest sideline. The sharp angle of the wide receiver's cut on this route makes it difficult for the defenders to prevent a completion.

■ COMEBACK

A 'comeback' route is a pass route that calls for the receiver to run down the field and then turn and run back toward the quarterback. This results in the receiver and the ball coming toward each other head-on, and therefore is a difficult type of route to defend against.

■ HITCH

A 'hitch' is a very quick, sharp, comeback move by the receiver, that can occur at the end of a pass route or be part of a combination route.

The pass routes illustrated are simple ones that give an idea of the types of routes you are likely to see. In actuality, a wide receiver may have twenty or more ways to run each of these routes, depending on the initial position of his defensive opponent and how his opponent reacts to him.

■ COMBINATION ROUTES

All of the routes we've just seen can be combined into routes with multiple moves. The more complex the route, the harder it is for the defender to stay with the receiver, but a receiver can often get tied up in a complicated route and never reach the spot where the quarterback expects him to be. The illustration shows two of the many possible 'combination' routes: a 'slant/flag' route being run by the split end, and a 'hitch-and-go' route by the flanker.

Most pass routes are designed for 'spot' passes; that is, to get the receiver to a particular spot on the field at the same time as the football arrives from the quarterback.

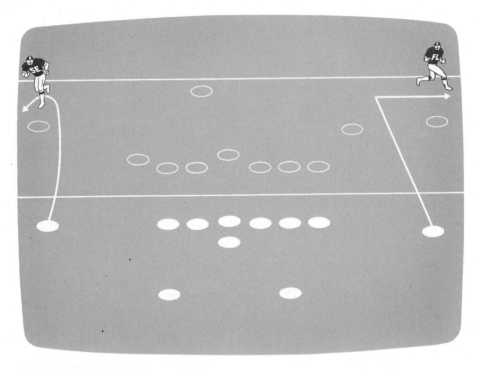

Pass Receiving

So far we've been watching the wide receivers run pass routes so that they can get to the spot on the field where the quarterback is aiming his pass. Now the wide receiver has to come up with the football. In order to do this, he can't rely on just his speed. He must coordinate his eyes, hands, arms, legs, and stomach so that he brings in the football for a completed pass.

■ SIDELINE ROUTES

Any route that ends up using the sideline is a 'sideline' route. It is difficult for the defender to stop this type of route, as the wide receiver is using the sideline as his ally. The defender can't get to the outside of the wide receiver, so he can only defend from three sides rather than four, and it is even difficult for the defenders to 'double-team' a wide receiver who is using the sideline as part of his pass route.

In our example, the split end is running a comeback route to the sideline and the flanker is running a post/square-out.

Sideline routes are often used so the wide receiver can go out of bounds and stop the clock during the final minutes of the half or game.

■ WATCHING THE BALL

The most basic rule for receivers is "Watch the ball!" The wide receiver can do everything else right — he can run a perfect pattern, trick his defender, and get by him — and still drop the pass because he has not watched the ball right into his hands. When you see a receiver drop a pass you can almost bet that he didn't keep his eyes on the football.

If, however, the receiver turns and looks for the ball too soon, it will reduce his speed and tip off his defender, or he may not get to the ball at all. Pass routes are timed with the quarterback so that if everything goes as planned, the ball will get to the receiver just as he has hit the right spot on the field. The wide receiver must have confidence in his quarterback and wait to look for the ball when he knows it should be there.

■ CATCHING THE BALL

A good receiver won't put his arms up to catch a pass before the ball has reached him. If he does this, he'll impede his maneuverability. All the great wide receivers have great 'extension'; that is, they can leap high and reach in any direction to come down with the pass.

There is also a right and wrong way for the wide receiver to use his hands when catching a pass. If a receiver tenses his hands the ball may bounce right off. The receiver must 'accept' the ball. Many receivers who have a high percentage of pass completions or who make difficult catches are said to have 'good hands'.

One common cause of dropped passes is the tendency of receivers to start to turn and run for further yardage with the football before they have actually caught it and tucked it away. You'll see this in practically every game you watch.

The Tight End

Now we're going to watch one of the least understood and yet one of the most exciting and talented players on the offensive squad: the tight end. The tight end has to be versatile. On some plays he must block on the line using the techniques of the interior linemen. Other times a play calls for him to go deep into the defensive backfield and block like a running back. He must also be able to run pass patterns and come up with pass receptions like a wide receiver.

In order to play all these roles, the tight end must have almost contradictory abilities. He should have the strength and size of an interior lineman, the running power of a running back, and the speed and agility of a wide receiver. We waited until now to watch him because he combines the jobs of all these positions.

■ COMING DOWN IN BOUNDS

Professional football rules require that a receiver come down with both feet in bounds and the football in his possession in order for a pass to be ruled complete. (In college football, the receiver need land with only one foot in bounds.) Being able to catch a sideline pass and then come down with both feet in bounds is an essential requirement for a wide receiver. This skill obviously requires both agility and an uncanny sense of timing.

If a wide receiver leaps and catches a pass in the air but is pushed by the defender out of bounds, it can still be considered a reception if, by the judgment of the official, the wide receiver could have landed in bounds.

■ THE TIGHT END (RIGHT SIDE)

The tight end can line up on either side of the interior line. If he lines up on the right side, you'll see three players to the right of the center and two to the left. In this situation the last man, or the outside man, on the right side of the line is the tight end.

This position for the tight end is the one we have been using for our illustrations throughout this book.

Remember that the side of the field with the tight end is called the 'strong side' and the opposite side the 'weak side'.

■ THE TIGHT END (LEFT SIDE)

The tight end can also line up on the left side of the interior line. Always look for the side of the line that has three linemen rather than two. The third man away from the center is the tight end. If the tight end is lined up on the left side, remember that the left side is now the strong side.

Also keep in mind that the wide receiver on the tight end side of the formation is the flanker, and that he must line up a yard behind the line of scrimmage.

Tight End Blocking

Since we've watched the interior linemen execute their line blocks and since we've also watched the running backs help on running plays with open field blocking, you now should enjoy watching the tight end block. You'll see him block off the line like an interior lineman as well as moving off the line to lead interference for the ball carrier, depending on the type of play called by the quarterback. You might want to review these blocks by skipping back to the interior line and running back sections. Remember, it is blocking that both sets up running plays and gives the quarterback time to throw accurate passes for receptions.

■ DOUBLE-TEAM BLOCK

Although you might see any two linemen using a double-team block, it is a standard block for the tight end on an off tackle play to the strong side, which is used to get one defender out of the way. On this block, the strong side tackle and tight end join forces to drive the defensive man back off the line of scrimmage. One offensive man acts as a 'post' and the other as a 'wheel' or 'drive'. In other words, one offensive man pushes the defensive man backwards and off balance as the other offensive man spins him to the left or right.

Tight End Pass Routes

There is essentially no difference between the pass routes run by the tight end and the routes run by the wide receivers, especially in pro football. The tight end must be able to run short, medium, and long routes. Tight ends run in's, out's, flags, and posts—everything. We'll look here at two special routes frequently run by the tight end.

Some people think that the tight end's routes are more difficult than those run by the wide receivers. This is so in part because the rules of the game allow any eligible receiver lined up within two yards of the offensive tackles to be blocked below the waist at the line of scrimmage. (A receiver who is lined up wide cannot be blocked below the waist unless he is carrying the ball or lead blocking.) Also, many of the tight end's pass routes are run to the center of the field and therefore call for him to catch the football in heavy traffic.

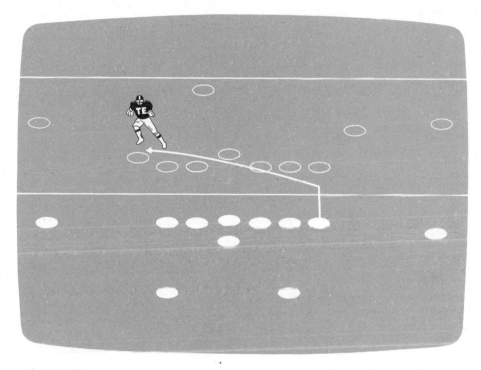

■ CROSS

One route often run by the tight end is the 'cross', in which the tight end streaks across the field parallel to the offensive line. This is also called a 'look-in' route.

The cross route is sometimes combined with a cross route in the opposite direction by the split end. This criss-cross by the two players makes defensive pass coverage difficult.

Pass Patterns

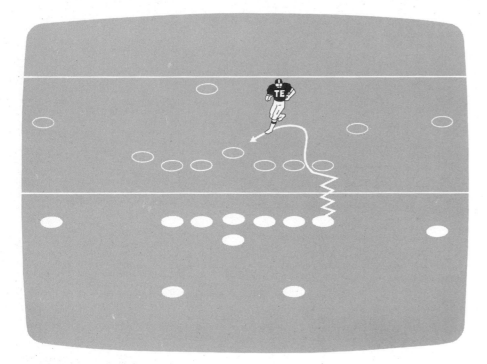

■ DELAY—HOOK

Since the defense knows that the tight end is used as an important blocker on running plays, the tight end often delays his pass route by faking as if to block and then taking off on his route. Sometimes he will even fall to the ground, pretending he has been blocked.

These 'delay' routes are used to try and fool the defense, and can be combined with other types of routes.

Our illustration shows a delay with a comeback being run to the 'hook' zone area of the field.

We've now watched the running backs, wide receivers, and the tight end run all the basic pass routes. Although we've looked at these positions and routes separately, you should realize by now that on each passing play, most, if not all of these eligible receivers will be running pass routes. These individual routes can be combined into an infinite variety of pass patterns.

When we look at our playbook in the Third Quarter, we'll see that these pass patterns can be designed to achieve different results, and that the choice of a particular pass pattern will also depend on what the defense is expected to do. For now, we'll simply review the individual routes that make up the arsenal of the passing game.

■ PASS ROUTE TREES

Here are the routes we've looked at so far, grouped into pass route 'trees'. Receivers practice their pass patterns by imagining these trees on the field and running the various routes. The coaches and quarterback will also plan and prepare for the passing game by thinking in terms of these pass route trees.

It's very important to keep in mind that, while we've grouped the routes into those frequently run by the wide receivers, tight end, and running backs, any player might run any route, or a combination of these routes, on a particular play.

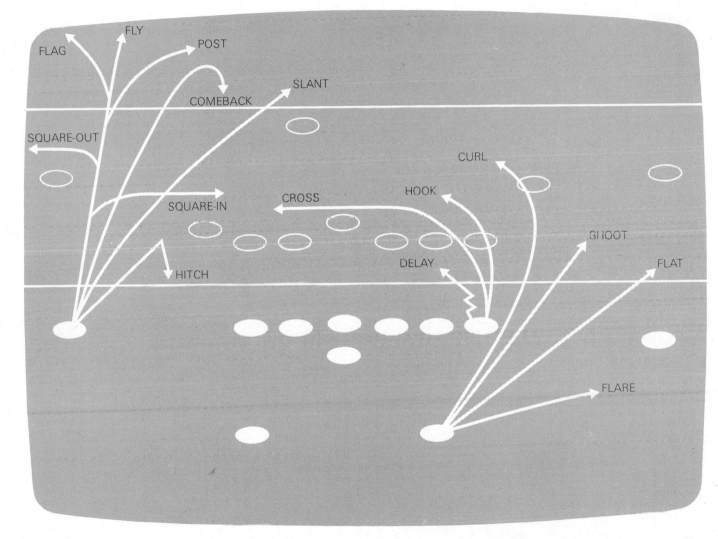

The Quarterback

We're finally going to take a look at the player who has been setting in motion all the activity we've been watching: the quarterback. The quarterback receives more attention by far from the TV camera and the commentators than any other position. Considering his importance to the offensive game plan and its execution, it's probably justified that the quarterback is considered the star of the show.

Nevertheless, the quarterback can, at best, only coordinate the skills of his offensive teammates. The quarterback needs tough linemen to provide running and passing block protection, strong running backs to hand off to, swift wide receivers to snare his passes, and the triple-threat tight end.

■ FIELD GENERAL

The quarterback is in charge of the entire offensive team. Whether or not he chooses the play, it's his job to communicate that play to the rest of the team. He also has the power to change the play called if he doesn't like the way the defense lines up. He calls the signals that set the play in motion, and he starts the play by receiving the snap from the center.

Once the quarterback has the ball, he'll either hand it off to a running back, throw a pass to a receiver, or, occasionally, keep the ball and run with it himself. We're going to watch the quarterback do all these jobs before the end of this First Quarter.

◼ PLAY SELECTION

There are two methods for selecting the play. The decision is either made on the sideline or by the quarterback.

When the play is called from the sideline, it is often the result of a complicated process. High in the stadium, near where the TV commentators sit, are two coaching booths, one for each team. Each team has three or four assistant coaches in its booth, who communicate information about the game to assistant coaches on the sidelines through headphones. They, in turn, pass this information on to the team's offensive and defensive coordinators, who may then consult with the head coach and decide what play to call. Finally, a player is sent into the huddle to pass on this play to the quarterback. Some teams use hand signals to communicate plays to the quarterback, although this risks having the code broken by the other team.

Some teams, however, let their quarterback call the plays. These teams reason that since he is in the thick of the

game he'll know better what play the situation calls for. Information from the booth may still be sent in to the quarterback, but the quarterback makes the final decision.

(All of what we have said about picking the play has not covered the mass of information involved in the strategic decisions regarding the play selection. We'll devote the Fourth Quarter to strategy and the entire decision-making process.)

Once the play is selected, the quarterback must communicate the play to the other ten offensive players in the huddle. He must be concise and precise. In professional football the offensive team is allowed 30 seconds to go into the huddle, decide on its play, come out and set in its formation, and snap the football to start the play. (In college games, this must be accomplished in 25 seconds.) If the team exceeds this 30-second limitation, it will be penalized and the ball moved back.

Each team has therefore developed codes that quickly and accurately communicate the play in the offensive huddle. These codes differ from team to team, but they all use combinations of numbers, letters, colors, and other symbols to signify specific plays. Once this code has been called in the huddle, each offensive player knows exactly his assignment and on what signal the play will begin. For example, the quarterback might say, "Twenty-eight Pitch, on three," which might mean a pitch to the halfback, who will run through the number eight hole, with the play beginning on the count of three.

■ **AUDIBLES AND SIGNAL CALLING**

Once the play has been called in the huddle, the quarterback can still change his mind, based on what he sees when he comes out of the huddle. Suppose, for example, the quarterback has called a pitch play to the strong side. As he sets up in the offensive formation, he sees the defensive players shaded toward the strong side, anticipating a running play in that direction. After having read this defensive move, the quarterback wouldn't want to go ahead with that play; so at this point he might yell out a change of play, called a 'check off' or 'audible'.

An audible is simply the quarterback calling out a new play to his teammates at the line of scrimmage. The audible can change the play that was previously called in the huddle, or it can be an originally called play if the offensive team was told in the huddle to check for the play at the line of scrimmage.

Here's how the audible works. Just before the quarterback calls his signal for the snap of the ball, he will 'indicate' to the rest of the team if the play has been changed from the one called in the huddle, by calling a 'change indicator'. For example, the change indicator might be a "three." If the quarterback called "Three-ninety-nine," the "three" would indicate a change and the new play would be "ninety-nine." If, on the other hand, he called "Two-ninety-nine," the "two" would be a 'fake audible'; the play would proceed as originally called.

In a simplified form, here is how signal calling works. Suppose the offense has been told in the huddle that the play will start on a 'three count'. When he starts to call his signals, the quarterback will first say "set" so the players are prepared and take their set positions. He would then yell out, "Hut, hut, hut," or "Go, go, go." On the third "hut" or "go," the center snaps the ball, and the play begins.

The quarterback must develop a rhythm or cadence that is easily recognized by his team so that they will not jump too soon and end up with an off-side penalty, but the quarterback must also be able to mix up the rhythm and final count of his call so that the defense can't anticipate the snap and get a jump on the offense.

By varying his cadence and the number of words in the series and communicating this change to his offensive team, the quarterback may be able to pull the defense offside. Suppose that the quarterback usually uses the cadence "Hut, hut-hut," but on one play he goes "Hut-hut, hut." This change in cadence might confuse the defense into moving forward too soon.

The quarterback must always call his signals and audibles loudly and clearly because it is crucial that his teammates be able to hear him. This is why when fans are noisy the quarterback will raise his hands to quiet them or even ask an official to call an official's time out until the crowd calms down. (The effect of the crowd does tend to give the home team some advantage.)

The Quarterback: Running Plays

The skills the quarterback uses depend on whether the play is a run or a pass. As we'll see, the quarterback is an integral part of both types of plays. Let's first watch the moves that the quarterback uses to help spring loose the ball carrier on running plays.

■ **RECEIVING THE SNAP**

At the selected count, the quarterback will receive the ball from the center. This requires much practice and great coordination between the center and the quarterback. Now that we're watching the quarterback, you might want to turn back to the section on the center and review this exchange. The exchange between the quarterback and center is practiced on a daily basis. If their timing is just a hair off, it could foul up the rhythm of the play, leading to a broken play — or a disastrous fumble. While this snap may look simple enough when you're watching the game, the success of each play depends on its perfection.

■ HIDING THE BALL

When we watched the running backs, we saw that the quarterback either handed off the football directly to a running back or faked a handoff to one running back and then actually handed off to another. In order to make the fake handoff even more effective, the quarterback learns to hide the ball on the back of his hip so the defense is even more inclined to think it is in the running back's arms. If the quarterback is clever at this deception the defense will converge on the wrong man. We will also see, when watching the quarterback on passing plays, that he'll sometimes hide the football after faking to both running backs and then pass it downfield.

■ PITCHING OUT

Rather than handing off the ball to a running back on a running play, you may see the quarterback pitch out the ball to the running back. In pro ball, there are two types of pitch-outs the quarterback will use: the spiraling lateral and the dead ball lateral. We also watched this exchange in detail in the ball-handling part of the running back section, so you already should be familiar with how the running backs receive the ball.

As you watch the pitch-out, notice that the running back often is running at full speed when the quarterback pitches out the ball to him. This means the quarterback has to 'lead' the running back so he can catch it on the dead run and continue toward his running hole.

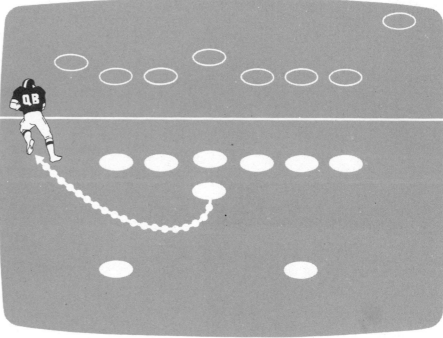

■ QUARTERBACK SNEAK

If only short yardage is needed, and especially if no defender is lined up in front of the center, the quarterback will sometimes take the ball and 'sneak', or dive forward, with the center or a guard leading for him. This is called the 'quarterback sneak', or 'keeper', and is regarded as just about the safest play in football. There is no handoff involved, so there is little danger of a fumble if the quarterback cradles the football with both hands and arms as he goes through the line.

A variation on the sneak is the 'quarterback draw', in which the quarterback takes the snap and first drops back as if to pass. He then quickly runs up the middle past the pass-rushing defense.

■ BOOTLEG

On this tricky maneuver, the quarterback fakes a handoff to a running back and hides the ball on his hip. He then runs in the opposite direction of the faked play. He can either keep the ball and run himself, pitch it out to another running back, or pass. The purpose of this move is to deceive the defense and, hopefully, catch them leaving open a running hole or passing opportunity.

The Quarterback: Passing Plays

On passing plays, you will see the quarterback get himself positioned to release the football, set up, and throw. These all involve important techniques that the quarterback has to have down pat in order to make the passing offense work. All quarterbacks have individual styles and favorite ways of engineering the passing attack, but perhaps the most important qualities that a passing quarterback must have are courage and trust. He must have the courage to stand there in the backfield unafraid of the onrushing defensive players and trust in his offensive line to protect him from this onslaught.

■ DROPPING BACK

Most quarterbacks use the 'drop-back' technique before passing the football. First the quarterback takes the snap from the center. Then he back-pedals, looking downfield in the direction of his receivers. After getting back, the quarter back stops, 'sets up', and prepares to fire.

Quarterbacks use this technique because it allows their linemen and running backs to form a protective pocket around them. It also gives the quarterback time to locate a receiver and

pass, and allows the receivers to get further downfield on long pass plays.

While the quarterback is dropping back, he will be 'reading' the defense, which means watching the movement of the defensive players in order to detect the type of pass coverage and find the best passing target. We'll see this clearly in the Second Quarter when we watch the defensive pass coverage and in the Third Quarter when we look at passing plays.

■ ROLLING OUT

Some quarterbacks prefer to 'roll out', or sprint out, as they prepare to throw a pass. When a quarterback rolls out, he takes the snap from the center and runs to his right or left while looking downfield for a receiver. One advantage to the roll-out technique is that the quarterback may get a better angle to pass over the defenders, who, as we'll soon see, are likely to be very tall.

Generally, right-handed quarterbacks tend to roll out to the right and left handers to the left.

One liability to the roll-out is that the quarterback is not protected by a pocket of teammates, although the offensive line and running backs will try to roll out with the quarterback to give him some protection. Quarterbacks who want the option of running with the football themselves will also use the roll-out to look for a running hole to scramble through.

■ THE SHOTGUN

We're soon going to look at many alternative formations, but we'll take a look now at one of them, the 'shotgun', because it's in part an alternative to the dropback.

In this formation, the quarterback, or 'trigger' of the 'shotgun', starts the play about seven yards behind the center and receives the ball from him on the fly. The quarterback drops back a couple more yards, sets up, and shoots a pass downfield to the receivers.

This technique is not used by many teams because the shotgun formation tips off the defense to a certain passing play, and because the on-the-fly exchange between the center and quarterback is more dangerous than the usual center snap. The shotgun does, however, allow the quarterback to look downfield from the instant he gets the snap and doesn't require as much pass block protection time from the linemen.

■ PASSING

Once the quarterback has found his target, he must be able to spiral the football to that receiver, wherever he may be on the field. Sometimes the quarterback must 'lead' the receiver so he can catch the pass on the run, or throw the ball low to keep it away from pass defenders.

Just as the quarterback had to be able to fake a handoff, he must be able to fake the direction of his passes. He'll do this with his head and eyes by looking in the opposite direction from where he will throw the ball. This is known as 'looking off' the pass defenders. He'll also pump his arm as though he is throwing a pass in one direction and then throw it somewhere else.

Finally, the quarterback must have a good 'touch' with the football. One play may call for a bullet and the next play for a feather. It is often the touch and accuracy of the quarterback's passes that give great receivers their reputations.

■ DUMPING THE BALL

If the quarterback drops back to pass, finds all his receivers covered, no 'safety valve' receiver to pass to, his blockers providing him no pocket, and looks straight into the faces of two 250-pound defenders who are about to flatten him, what does he do with the football?

In this situation the quarterback must stay calm and throw the ball on the ground, out of bounds, or out of reach of everyone, so that he doesn't get tackled, or 'sacked', and lose yardage. His throwing the ball away, or 'dumping' the football, will be an incomplete pass, and the next play will begin from the original line of scrimmage. The quarterback must make it look like he is really aiming his pass for an eligible receiver, as his team can be penalized for 'intentional grounding'. As long as the throw-away pass comes reasonably close to an eligible receiver, however, intentional grounding usually is not called.

Offensive Formation Variations

So far, we have looked at the three 'Set' formations and the I Formation. You'll see these formations most often if you are watching a professional game. These formations also are used by many college teams. We'll now look at some other commonly used formations that are variations on the formations we've been watching. We'll see that different formations favor particular types of plays and are used depending on the game situation.

A formation can be changed three ways. There are variations that involve the positions of the running backs, those that alter the position of the flanker, and variations in the players on the line of scrimmage. Combining these variations gives all the formations possible.

■ SHIFTS AND MOTION

Have you noticed that after the offense has lined up in its formation and the quarterback has started calling his signals, the two running backs sometimes appear to be jumping back and forth from one formation to another? All they are doing with these backfield 'shifts' is trying to confuse the defense. However much switching they do, the rules say that all the players on the line, and all but one backfield player, must be 'set', or perfectly still, for one second before the play begins.

The one backfield player who does not have to be set can be used as a 'man in motion'. He can move while the quarterback is calling the signals, so long as he does not move forward or toward the line of scrimmage prior to the snap of the ball. Most often you will see the flanker as the man in motion. This move, too, is designed to confuse the defense and thus get a jump on them.

Running Back Variations

All the following offensive formation variations simply adjust the positions of the running backs. These positions of the running backs can be changed to give an advantage to either a running or passing attack.

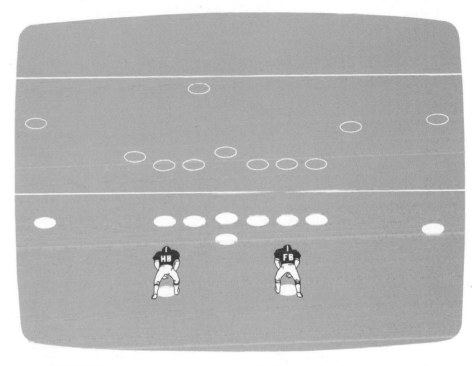

■ **OPEN SET**

The Open Set formation is the first formation we looked at. It is often used for passing situations. In this formation, both running backs are lined up behind the offensive tackles. This also is called the 'Full Set', the 'Split Set', or, because it was first made popular by professional teams, the 'Pro Set'.

This is a good passing play formation because the positions of the running backs allow them either to take off past the line on a pass route or to provide the quarterback with protection when he drops back to pass.

The running back on the tight end side, or strong side, is the fullback and the running back on the weak side is the halfback.

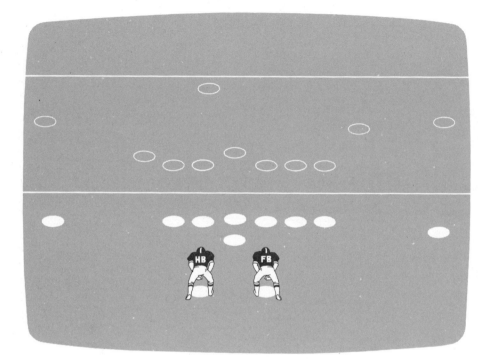

■ TWIN SET

This is a variation on the Open Set. In this formation the running backs are each lined up behind the offensive guards. This puts them so close together that the formation is known as the 'Twin Set'.

In this position the running backs are better able to lead block for each other on running plays, but have further to go to get out of the backfield, around the line, and out on a pass route. For this reason, you'll often see this formation used for running plays.

The running back on the tight end side is the fullback and the running back on the weak side is the halfback.

■ SPREAD SET

Notice in this running back variation that the running backs are spread so far apart they are to the outside of the interior line. In this position, they cannot provide good blocking support for each other, so think "pass" when you see this formation.

The running back on the tight end side is the fullback and the other running back is the halfback.

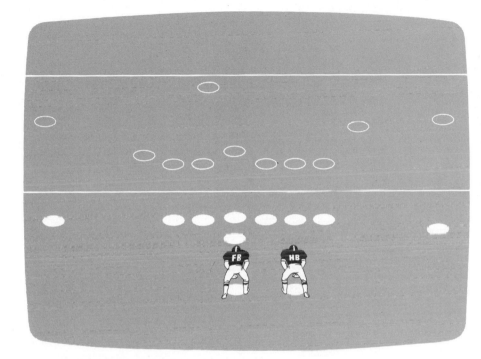

■ STRONG SIDE SET

This is another of the formations we've already looked at. The Strong Side Set favors a running play, especially a running play to the strong, or tight end, side. One running back, the fullback, is lined up directly behind the quarterback. The other running back, the halfback, is set up behind the strong side tackle. This also is called the Near Side Set, as the halfback is near the tight end.

■ WEAK SIDE SET

The Weak Side Set favors a run, to either the strong or the weak side. The running back behind the quarterback is the fullback and the running back behind the weak side tackle is the half-back. This is also called the Far Side Set, as the halfback is far from the tight end.

At first glance, these five formations (Open, Twin, Spread, Strong Side, and Weak Side) may be difficult to distinguish, especially if you are watching the game on TV. If you can learn to spot them, however, you can often get a jump on following the play.

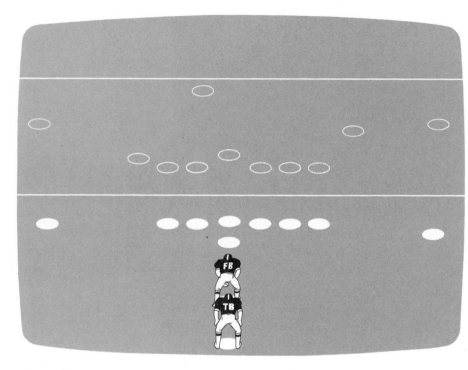

■ I FORMATION

We also looked at this formation at the beginning of the quarter. The fullback lines up directly behind the quarterback, and the tailback lines up behind the fullback, forming the letter 'I'.

This is a good running play formation. The positions of the backs make it difficult for the defense to spot handoffs clearly, and to tell which back has the ball. The fullback is in a good position to run with the ball by himself or to lead block for the tailback. The tailback's upright stance also gives him a better view of the defense and potential running holes.

■ SINGLE SET BACK

This formation moves one of the running backs out of the backfield and up to a yard behind the line, while the other running back remains in the backfield. This formation predicts a passing play.

The running back in the backfield is called the 'set back'. He can line up to the right or left of the quarterback, or sometimes directly behind him, and provides blocking protection. The running back who has moved forward generally lines up in the area between the weak side tackle and the split end, called the 'slot', and for this reason is called the 'slot back' (SB). From his position close to the line he can get downfield quickly to receive a pass.

This formation provides, in effect, three wide receivers. Frequently, the player who lines up in the slot will, in fact, be a wide receiver player, rather than a running back.

Flanker Variations

The flanker can leave his position on the far strong side of the formation and do one of three things. He can stay on his side of the field and line up a yard behind but near the tight end; he can stay a yard behind the line of scrimmage but move over to the split end side of the field; or he can join the running backs in the backfield. These changes will alert you to various formations that you are sure to see as you watch the game.

As these formations change, it is also possible that the offensive personnel will change. In other words, the flanker may not actually move to the backfield to become a running back; instead a running back player may replace the flanker in the backfield.

■ WING SET

This is a simple flanker variation that is often used to set up a running play. The flanker moves from his normal position to a spot just outside the tight end, called the 'wing' position. Notice that the flanker remains a yard behind the offensive line so he is still in the backfield. When the flanker lines up this way he is sometimes called a 'wing back' (WB) and the formation is called a 'Wing Set'. This formation favors a running play.

(The ellipses at the top of each illustration represent the defensive players. Since the defense shifts in response to different offensive formations, we'll make appropriate adjustments in the next several diagrams. We'll cover the reasoning behind these shifts when we look at the defense in the Second Quarter.)

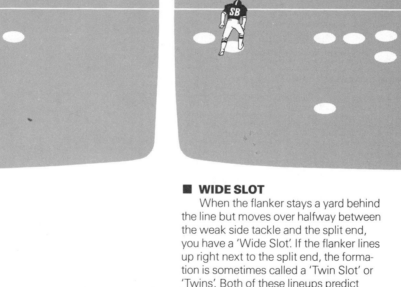

■ TIGHT SLOT

In the 'Tight Slot' formation the flanker stays a yard behind the line of scrimmage, but moves over so he is lined up just outside the offensive weak side tackle, to become a slot back. Most slot formations predict passing plays, but notice that this formation can be considered a 'two tight end' formation, which allows the offense to run with an equal amount of line blockers to both sides of the ball.

■ WIDE SLOT

When the flanker stays a yard behind the line but moves over halfway between the weak side tackle and the split end, you have a 'Wide Slot'. If the flanker lines up right next to the split end, the formation is sometimes called a 'Twin Slot' or 'Twins'. Both of these lineups predict a passing play, weighted to the 'slotted' side of the field.

You will very often see the flanker go in motion from his normal position, cross parallel to the line, and be ready to cut downfield for a pass from the slot as the ball is snapped.

■ POWER I

This is one of a number of formations in which the flanker moves into the backfield to become a third running back. In the Power I, the flanker's position is to the strong side of the fullback and tailback in their I Formation positions.

In a pro game, you'll sometimes see the flanker line up in this position and then go in motion as the signals are called. In short yardage situations, the flanker may actually be replaced at this position by an extra running back. The extra running back makes this a powerful running play formation.

■ FULL I

Here the flanker's position in the backfield presents another triple running back formation. The fullback is behind the quarterback and there are two tailbacks in back of him.

This is a running formation for short yardage or goal line situations. If the quarterback can execute a handoff deceptively it will be difficult for the defense to locate the ball carrier. This formation also yields the maximum lead blocking strength. This is primarily a college game formation.

■ WISHBONE T

Notice that the backfield of this formation looks like a wishbone. The back behind the quarterback is a fullback and the other two are halfbacks. This is also a running formation which is used successfully by many college teams.

■ T FORMATION

Here, the three running backs are lined up behind the quarterback in nearly a straight line. The one in the middle is a fullback while the two on the outside are halfbacks. With the quarterback in front, the backfield resembles the letter 'T'.

Although our illustration does not show it, the traditional lineup for this formation moved the split end in to become another tight end on the line.

This formation favors a running attack and, before the importance of the passing game, was football's most used formation.

Line Variations

Remember, the rules of football say that there must be at least seven players on the line of scrimmage. It is extremely rare to have more than seven players on the line of scrimmage, since all the backfield players are eligible to receive passes but only the two end men on the line are eligible. A team would give up a passing advantage by pulling more than seven players on the line. For this reason, virtually all line variations still involve five interior linemen and two ends

■ TWO TIGHT ENDS

The split end does not have to split out to the weak side. He can remain on the line but move in tight next to the interior linemen. If this happens he is usually replaced by a tight end player. When you hear a commentator say, "There are two tight ends," this is the line formation he is talking about.

This formation is a good tip-off that the play is going to be a running play. The split end has moved over to give extra blocking power to the line. (This was the standard lineup for the old T Formation.)

In recent years, some teams have successfully utilized this two-tight-end formation for a passing attack when there were weaknesses at the wide receiver position.

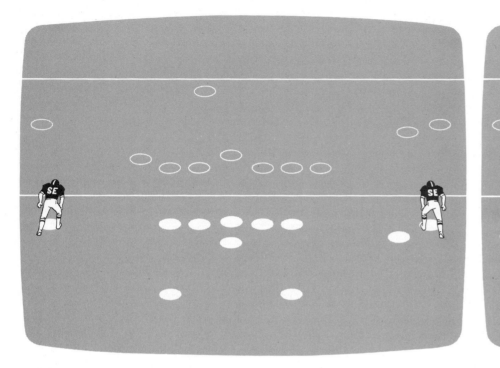

■ TWO SPLIT ENDS

Here, the tight end moves over wide to the strong side to become another split end. When this happens, it is possible that he will be replaced by a wide receiver player. The flanker remains in his normal position, actually in a 'slot' with the new split end.

This is another 'three-wide-receiver' formation that signals an attempt for a long pass. You're likely to see this type of formation when a team needs quick, long yardage, especially toward the end of the game.

■ UNBALANCED LINE

This final line variation is one that you'll occasionally see in college ball. The line is said to be 'unbalanced' because there are more interior linemen to one side of the center than the other. Notice that in our illustration there are two tight ends, with the flanker split to the weak side and the running backs in a Strong Side Set.

A team will sometimes employ this type of formation to compensate for a weakness in its line personnel, or simply to throw the defense off balance.

Combining Variations

If you combine the running back, flanker, and line variations we've just looked at, you can come up with all the formations you will ever see. Here are some variations you are likely to encounter in professional games.

■ STRONG SIDE SET—TWIN SLOT

This is a 'balanced' formation; that is, the left side has potentially the most receivers and poses the stronger passing threat, but the right side has the most blocking help and ball carriers and is the strong running side. (The side with the tight end is still the 'strong side' according to the standard terminology.)

■ TWO TIGHT ENDS—WING— I FORMATION

This is a likely running formation. Not only are both ends tight and the two running backs in an I behind the quarterback, but the flanker has moved over near the tight end as a wing back. The whole offensive team is grouped for a run up the middle.

■ DOUBLE WING

This is a sure running formation that you might see in a short yardage or goal line situation. Both ends are tight, the flanker has moved over to become a wing back, and one running back has moved to the tight slot position to become another wing back. The running back behind the quarterback will get the ball and try to locate a hole in the hope of picking up a yard or two.

■ TRIPS

Our final combining formation not only commits the offense to pass, but also telegraphs the direction of its passing attack by putting three wide receiver players on the same side of the formation. Notice that the weak side of this formation is staffed by the split end, who is playing his normal position, and by two other wide receiver types, who are both playing in the slot. This type of formation is frequently called 'Trips', since there is a triple-wide-receiver threat on one side of the field.

This setup is often used when there is little time left in the game and the offense must throw the long bomb in a desperate try for a touchdown. The three receivers will usually try to 'flood', or converge on the same area of the field, hoping that one of them will come up with a reception.

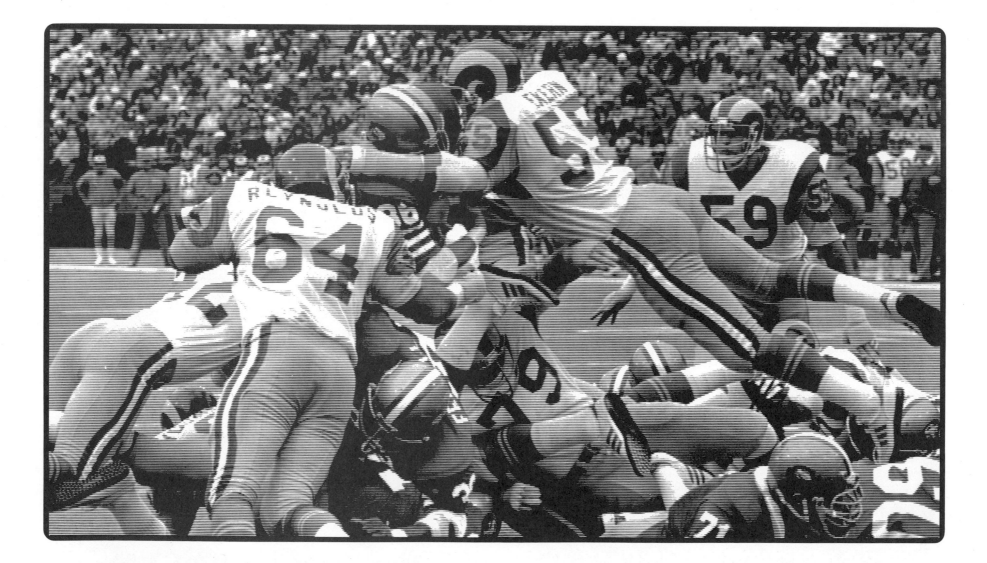

2ND QUARTER

Watching the Defense and Special Teams

While the teams are exchanging sides of the field for the start of the Second Quarter, let's take a minute to explode the myth that the offense is more interesting to watch than the defense. Television has coaxed us into this misunderstanding by giving so much coverage to the running backs and wide receivers and, especially, to the quarterback. But by the end of this quarter we should understand that, even though the TV director may not think so, the defense may be more interesting to watch than the offense.

Consider what the defensive players face on every play. They have to try to guess what the offensive play will be, decide on the defensive moves they will use to foil the play, and then be prepared to react to a completely different situation being thrown at them by an offensive squad doing its utmost to deceive them. This is why the best athletes, if not the best-known athletes, are often on the defensive squad. Defense is the key to winning football.

In case you've been wondering what to watch when one team kicks off, punts, or attempts a field goal or extra point, we'll be ending this Second Quarter by watching the special teams who take the field on all kicking situations.

Defensive Alignments and Positions

Just as we began the First Quarter by looking at basic offensive formations, we'll begin this quarter by watching how the defense lines up to oppose the offensive play. Defensive formations are called 'alignments' and the two most commonly used alignments are what are called the '4-3 Defense' and the '3-4 Defense'. You'll see that the names of some of the players change as the defensive alignment changes.

As you watch the game, you'll see that the defense is often in constant motion before the play begins. The defensive men jump around or shift to position themselves just prior to the snap of the ball, and at first this may give you the impression that there is no definite alignment at all. Stick with us and soon you'll be able to spot the difference between the '4-3' and '3-4', as well as identifying some other defensive alignment subtleties.

■ THE 4-3 DEFENSE

The '4-3' Defense is one of the most common defensive alignments. What do those numbers mean? Most defensive alignments are identified by numbering systems that tell you how many of each of the three basic types of defensive players there are in the game at the start of a play.

In the 4-3 Defense, there are four players, generally closest to the football, who start out with one or both hands on the ground in what is called a 'down' stance. These players are called the 'down linemen' and they make up the 'defensive line'. Their job is to oppose the blocks of the offensive line so that they can get to the ball carrier or passer.

The next three players are the 'linebackers', so called because they generally back up the line, although you will see them playing alongside the down linemen as well. Whether they play just behind or on the line, they will be in an upright or semi-crouch stance. The linebackers defend mainly against runs and short passes by the offense.

The final four players are called 'defensive backs', or, often, the 'secondary'. They usually play further back than the linebackers, and start out in an upright stance. The secondary mainly defends against passes, although we will see that they also have responsibilities on running plays.

The 4-3 Defense gets its name from the fact that there are four down linemen and three linebackers playing for the defense. Occasionally, the secondary players are included in the numbering system, and you'll hear this defense referred to as the '4-3-4'. You'll also sometimes hear this called an 'Even' defense, meaning that there are an even number of down linemen. In any case, the key to spotting this defense is to look for the four down linemen and three linebackers.

Now let's look at the names of the individual positions in this alignment: The four down linemen are made up of two linemen who play on the inside of the line, called 'defensive tackles' (DT), and two 'defensive ends' (DE), who are on each end of the line.

The three linebackers (LB) are comprised of a 'middle' linebacker and two 'outside' linebackers.

Two of the four secondary men play wide to each side and are called the 'cornerbacks' (CB). The remaining two secondary men are called 'safeties'. The one who plays on the strong side of the field (the side with the offensive tight end) is called the 'strong safety' (SS). The other safety is called the 'free safety' (FS), or sometimes the 'weak safety' since he lines up against the weak side of the offense.

Some teams prefer this 4-3 Defense while others prefer the next alignment we will look at, the 3-4 Defense. As we'll see, this preference is largely a matter of the team's personnel and the strategy of the defense. The 4-3 Defense is effective against both runs and passes, but, because there are more down linemen than linebackers, it is thought to defend slightly better against the run.

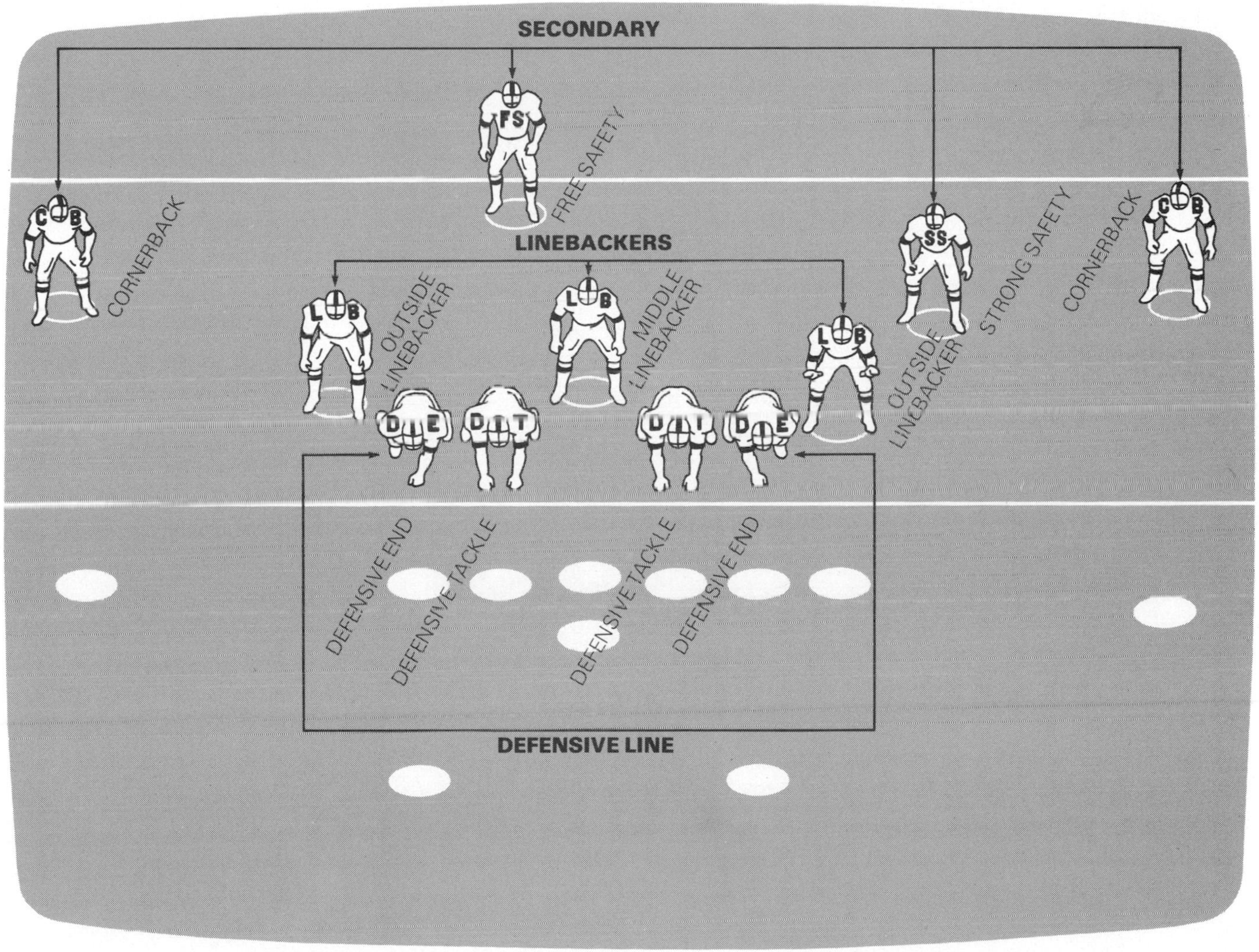

SECONDARY

FS

FREE SAFETY

CORNERBACK

LINEBACKERS

LB

OUTSIDE LINEBACKER

LB

MIDDLE LINEBACKER

LB

SS

OUTSIDE LINEBACKER

STRONG SAFETY

CORNERBACK

DE DT DT DE

DEFENSIVE END

DEFENSIVE TACKLE

DEFENSIVE TACKLE

DEFENSIVE END

DEFENSIVE LINE

■ THE 3–4 DEFENSE

Instead of having four down linemen and three linebackers, the 3–4 Defense has three down linemen and four linebackers. The one new name to learn is the 'nose guard'. He is the down lineman in the middle who is lined up 'nose-to-nose' with the center. And, instead of one middle linebacker, there are two 'inside'

linebackers. This is sometimes called an 'Odd' defense, because there are an odd number of down linemen.

These are the names of the players in the 3–4 Defense: The three down linemen are the 'nose guard' (NG) and two 'defensive ends' (DE).

The four linebackers (LB) are comprised of two 'inside' linebackers and two 'outside' linebackers.

The secondary is the same as in the

4–3 Defense: two cornerbacks (CB) and a strong safety (SS) and free safety (FS).

The 3–4 Defense is also flexible against a running and passing offensive attack, but it is thought to be slightly more efficient against a pass because of the extra linebacker.

You are likely to see either the 4–3 Defense or the 3–4 Defense on most every play in a professional game, except in special situations. We'll look at some of these after we have watched all the defensive positions.

■ COVERAGE AND MATCHUPS

The concept of matchups can be best understood by looking at the illustration, which shows a typical height and weight for each offensive and defensive position, based on the rosters of professional teams. Of course, the skills of each player are crucial, but the heights and weights tell much of the story. The defense wouldn't want a 6′9″, 275-lb. defensive end trying to keep up with a 6′1″, 190-lb. wide receiver on a pass play, or a 6′, 208-lb. cornerback trying to block a 6′4″, 270-lb. offensive tackle on a running play. The individual defensive players, as well as the defensive alignments and the whole scheme of defensive play, are chosen so that defensive players will have a strength or speed matchup with the players they are expected to cover.

With these physical qualities in mind, let's look at basic 'man-for-man' defensive coverage, with the 4–3 Defense against the Open Set Formation:

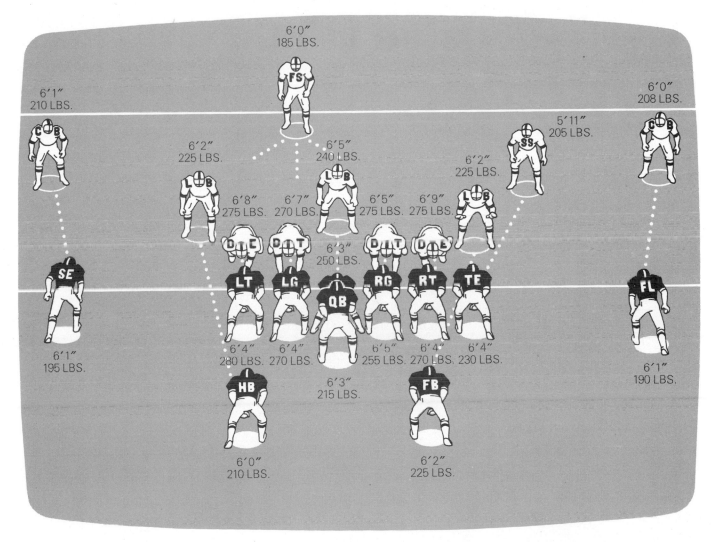

• The two defensive tackles are matched against the two offensive guards.

• The two defensive ends are matched against the two offensive tackles.

• The middle linebacker is matched against the center.

• The two outside linebackers cover the two running backs (halfback and fullback).

• The two cornerbacks cover the two wide receivers (split end and flanker).

• The strong safety covers the tight end.

• The free safety does not have a specific man to cover; he is free to help where needed.

We'll soon see that there is much more complexity to the defensive play than these man-for-man matchups. For instance, the line is usually defended according to responsibilities for 'gaps', or running holes, and passes are often defended against by various 'zone' systems. However, these matchups are an important start to understanding how the offense and defense interact.

The Defensive Line

We've already watched the offensive linemen performing their blocking duties. Now we'll look at their opponents in the trenches—the defensive line. As we will see, it is the struggle between these two groups of linemen that largely determines the outcome of both running and passing plays.

On each running play, the defensive linemen have specific areas or gaps to protect, depending on their assignments for the play, and it is the defensive linemen's job to keep those areas closed up. On passing plays, the defensive linemen will be trying to rush past the offensive linemen to get at the quarterback.

■ DOWN LINEMEN

We just saw that the number of defensive linemen varies according to the defensive alignment. Regardless of how many linemen there are, they are easy to distinguish from the linebackers who play behind or next to them. At the start of the play, the defensive linemen will be down in a 'three-' or 'four-point' stance; that is, with either one or both hands on the ground. This is why they are called 'down linemen' or, in the 4-3 Defense, the 'down four'. These down linemen are also sometimes called the 'front wall'. Their general duties are to fight through the pressure of the offensive blockers to get to the ball carrier or passer.

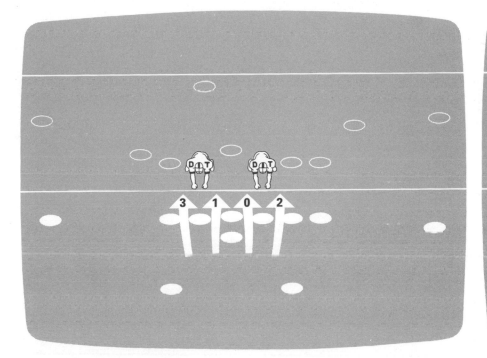

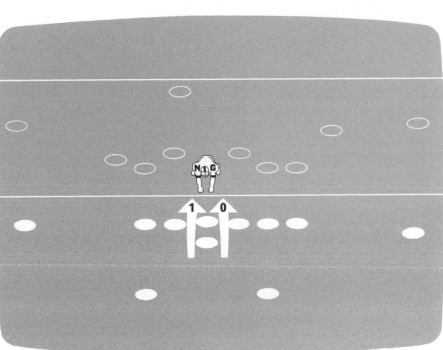

■ THE DEFENSIVE TACKLES

In the 4-3 Defense, the defensive tackles are matched against the offensive guards and may be called upon to defend two of the four inside running holes. (See page 37 of the First Quarter for an explanation of running holes and their numbering.)

The defensive linemen must always 'fight through pressure' on running plays. This means that they must not attempt to go around the blocks being thrown at them by the offense; they must stay put and fight through these blocks. The offense always will be trying to move a defensive lineman backwards or to one side in order to open up a running hole for the ball carrier. If the defensive lineman merely avoids the block by moving to the side he is being pushed, he is almost certainly giving up that hole to the offense.

Defensive tackles are drafted for their size and strength, as these are the basic tools they need in their fight with the offensive linemen.

■ THE NOSE GUARD

In the 3-4 Defense, the nose guard, or 'middle guard' as he is sometimes called, takes on much the same job as the two tackles in the 4-3 Defense. (You'll hear some commentators call him the 'nose tackle'.) He is matched against the center and, depending on his defensive play assignment, may be called upon to protect the running hole to either side of him. This is a big job, and you are likely to see an exceptionally big, tough player at this position.

Like the defensive tackles, the nose guard must fight through pressure, although some pro nose guards are so quick they can get around an offensive block and right at the ball carrier. On passing plays, the nose guard will be trying to get past the center to harass or sack the quarterback.

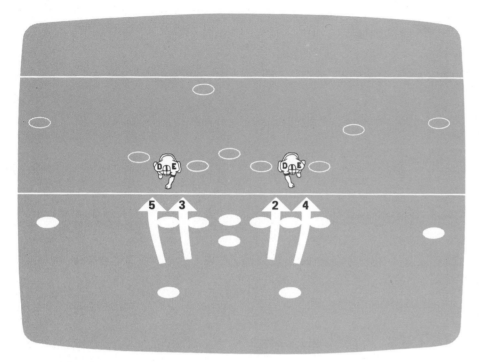

■ THE DEFENSIVE ENDS (4-3 DEFENSE)

In both the 4-3 and the 3-4 Defenses, the defensive ends are matched against the offensive tackles, and on running plays they may be called upon to protect two of the four running holes that are on either side of each of the two offensive tackles. They have essentially the same job as the defensive tackles and nose guard, except that the defensive ends have to help keep the ball carrier from going to the outside and breaking away. On passing plays the ends try to get past the offensive line to sack the quarterback.

In addition to the usual defensive line requirements of weight and strength, defensive ends must be mobile. They are also chosen for their height, as they frequently are rushing the quarterback from the angle where he'll find his wide receivers, and it creates just one more problem for the quarterback to have to throw over the defensive ends' heads and arms.

■ THE DEFENSIVE ENDS (3-4 DEFENSE)

The positions of the defensive ends and their area responsibilities are the same in the 3-4 Defense as in the 4-3 Defense, except that the ends have a slightly tougher job out of the 3-4 Defense, since there are no defensive tackles playing next to them.

In our diagrams, we have shown the defensive linemen protecting the gaps between the offensive linemen.

The defense sometimes uses 'man' rather than 'gap' blocking assignments, in which case the defensive lineman is responsible for an offensive man and the 'half gap' to either side of him.

You also may see the defensive linemen actually position themselves in the gaps between the offensive linemen rather than playing 'head up' as we have shown them.

Defensive Line Keys

Although the defensive linemen have specific areas to defend on running plays, they also 'read', or look for clues, or 'keys', that may give them a possible advantage over their offensive opponents. As we will see in the Fourth Quarter when we look at football strategy, one key as to whether the play will be a run or a pass play is the game situation. Another key for the defensive line is the offensive formation, as this can be some indication as to what type of play to expect. Other keys for the defensive line come from watching their opponent's game films, which may show them the offensive line's blocking strengths, weaknesses, and tendencies.

Even with such knowledge, the defensive linemen look for additional keys on each play to give them an edge on their rivals in the trenches.

■ THE SNAP

The basic key for the defensive linemen is the snap of the ball. Although the defensive linemen look straight ahead at their offensive opponents, their peripheral vision allows them to see the center's hand and the football. Once either moves, even by mistake, the play is on and the defensive linemen will move to attack their offensive opponents.

As in any struggle, he who hits first has the advantage. This is why the defensive lineman keys on the ball rather than on his offensive opponent. If the defender waited for his offensive opponent to move first, he would be hit first, since the offensive lineman knows the signal for the snap. By keying on the ball and moving forward when it moves, the defensive lineman is at least possibly even with his offensive opponent.

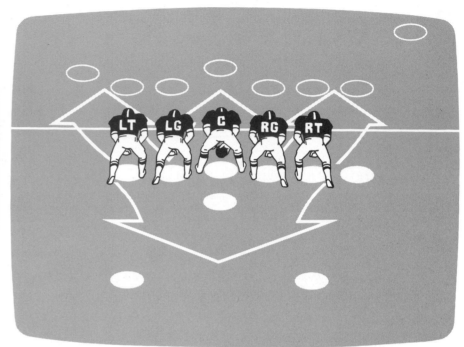

■ HELMETS

Once the ball has been snapped and the play has begun, the defensive linemen will key on the heads of the offensive men to get a clue as to the direction of the play. Whichever way the head goes, the body must follow. Defensive linemen are taught that if they fight 'across' the helmet of the opposing block, that key will lead them to the ball and a tackle.

■ PLAY FLOW

The defensive linemen also key on the same offensive line patterns we watched in the First Quarter. Since they are down with one or two hands on the ground they can't actually see the offensive movement, but they do 'feel' for it. If a defensive lineman feels the offensive line move straight forward after the ball is snapped, it is probably because the play is going forward. If the defensive lineman feels the offensive flow going to either side, he knows that most likely the play is going to that side. If the offensive line stands up and retreats, the play is likely to be a pass play.

One offensive movement that the defensive lineman can see is that of a pulling guard. If an offensive guard pulls back from the line and runs to either side, the defensive lineman (as well as we spectators) can expect an off tackle or outside play to that side.

Defensive Line Block Protection

The five offensive linemen execute the various blocking techniques that we watched in the First Quarter. But the defensive linemen have some tools of their own. They have a number of 'rushing', or 'block protection', techniques that help them fight off the offensive blocks. The particular techniques used will vary, depending on the way the play is moving and the offensive-defensive matchups, but the goal is always for the defensive men to defeat their offensive opponents and get to the ball carrier or passer.

It is very important to know that the defensive players are allowed to use their hands during block protection. They can even grab an offensive player to try and move him out of the way. But they cannot hold an offensive man (except when tackling the ball carrier).

■ SHIVER CHARGE

The 'shiver charge' allows the defensive lineman to fend off the charge of the offensive player. The defensive lineman slams his fists against the shoulders of the opposing lineman and tries to move him backwards. Leverage is important in this technique, as well as the fact that the defensive players are allowed to grab with their hands while the offense may not. If the defensive lineman can keep away from the offensive block, he will be free to react to the play and pursue the ball carrier or the passer.

■ SHOULDER LIFT

We have seen that the first responsibility of the defensive lineman is to protect his gap or running hole area. This is particularly important in the situation when the play is coming right at him. Now he knows he must close up the hole he is guarding. To do this he may use a 'shoulder lift'. Starting from his three- or four-point stance, the defensive lineman rises up and at the offensive man. The goal is to keep the offensive lineman from moving forward so that the running hole is jammed.

The defensive lineman must keep one arm free, on the side of the hole he is defending, so he can tackle a ball carrier who comes through that hole. Which hole he is to protect with his free arm is called in the defensive huddle. This is how he chooses between a left and right shoulder lift.

■ SUBMARINE

If a defensive lineman finds himself being double-team blocked by the offense, he will drop to the ground between the two offensive players so he *cannot* be removed from the offensive running lane. This makes sense, since if the defender is being double-teamed, the ball carrier is probably coming in his direction and the submarine will stack up the area. You also might see this tactic used if the offensive linemen have been charging with straight up or high blocks.

■ PASS RUSH

In the First Quarter we watched how the offensive linemen drop back to protect the quarterback on passing plays. The defense will try all kinds of moves in the battle against these pass blocks.

One such pass-rushing move is known as the 'swim technique'. While the offensive man is trying to stay between the quarterback and the defender, the defensive lineman tries to turn him with one arm and then swing his other arm over and around him, with a move that resembles an overhand crawl swimming stroke. Once the offensive player is turned out of position, the defender has a shot at the quarterback.

Sometimes the defenders will try an 'arm-under' move when they think their opponent is expecting the arm-over swim, or they'll grab the jersey of offensive man to try to turn him, or simply try to run straight over him with a move nicknamed the 'bull rush'.

■ SACKING THE QUARTERBACK

The pass rush is a crucial part of the defensive game. The more the quarterback is rushed, the less chance he has of completing his pass. The defensive line does its best to get at the quarterback quickly, before his receivers have run their patterns to their assigned spots on the field.

The ultimate goal of the pass rush is to force the quarterback out of his pocket of blockers and subject him to a punishing 'sack'. Tackling the quarterback with a sack ends the play, and spots the ball for the next play at the point of the sack. In addition, the quarterback has to suffer being knocked to the ground by one or more defenders. A quarterback sack also can be extremely demoralizing for the offensive linemen. Defensive linemen (and linebackers) take great pride in the number of quarterback sacks they can chalk up during a season.

The Linebackers

We're going to spend the next series of plays watching the men who back up the defensive line: the linebackers. The linebackers' job is perhaps the most demanding and exciting job on the defensive team. The linebacker position calls for almost contradictory abilities. The linebackers must be able to protect a specific area on running plays using the same block protection techniques as the defensive linemen. On passing plays, they must be able to rush the quarterback as well as to cover the offensive pass receivers. Finally, one of the linebackers acts as the field general of the defensive team.

The names used to describe the linebackers vary according to the defensive alignment, the linebackers' positions in a particular alignment, and their responsibilities or assignments.

■ **UPRIGHT STANCE**
The key to spotting the linebackers, regardless of the defensive alignment, is to watch the players closest to the line of scrimmage who are standing in an upright position, as opposed to being down in a three- or four-point stance. Although this upright, or 'two-point', stance is less stable than the down position used by the defensive linemen, it does give the linebackers a better view of a running play and more mobility for pass defense.

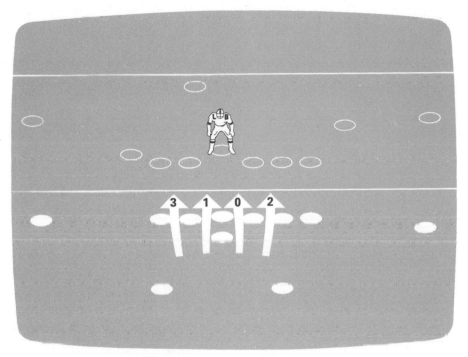

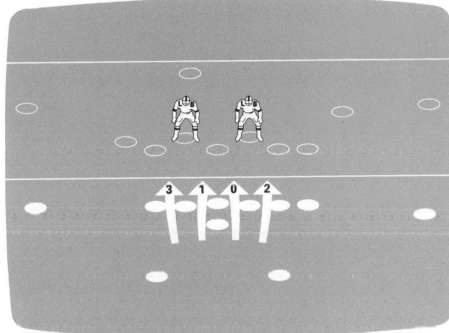

■ THE MIDDLE LINEBACKER (4-3 DEFENSE)

If the defense is in a 4-3 alignment, the linebacker in the middle is called the 'middle linebacker'. On running plays, depending on the particular play and the defensive gap responsibility scheme, he may be called upon to protect any one of the four inside holes between the two offensive tackles.

The middle linebacker is also the defensive captain, or field general for the defense. He is responsible for calling the defensive scheme to be used on each play in the defensive huddle, and for changing or adjusting that scheme if he does not like what he sees as the offense sets for the play.

The middle linebacker is also responsible for letting the defensive linemen know what type of formation the offense is in, usually by yelling out a color code word.

■ THE INSIDE LINEBACKERS (3-4 DEFENSE)

In the 3-4 Defense, there are two linebackers in the center of the defense, called the 'inside linebackers'. They back up the nose guard, and have responsibility for two of the same four inside running holes as the middle linebacker in the 4-3 Defense.

Usually, one of these inside linebackers will be the defensive captain, with the same defensive scheme responsibilities as the middle linebacker in the 4-3 Defense.

Linebacker Keys

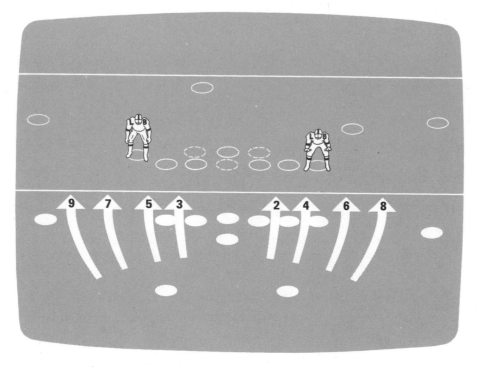

Earlier, we saw how the defensive linemen key, or read, the offense. The linebackers do the same, but their keys have somewhat greater scope than those of the defensive linemen, for two reasons.

First, the upright stance of the linebackers gives them a better view of the formation the offense sets in before the play, and a better view of the play as it develops. Second, the linebackers have to be prepared either to stop the ball carrier on running plays, or to drop back and provide pass defense on passing plays. (We'll look at pass defense in detail later in this Second Quarter.)

We'll look now at some important linebacker keys. These keys help the linebackers to follow the activity of the offense, so if we learn them they can also be very helpful to us as spectators.

■ THE OUTSIDE LINEBACKERS (4-3 AND 3-4 DEFENSES)

In both the 4-3 and 3-4 alignments, the two linebackers closest to each side-line are called the 'outside linebackers'. In either defense, the outside linebacker is called upon to protect one of the four outside running holes on his side of the field. The outside linebackers coordinate this gap defense in conjunction with the defensive ends and the secondary men, whom we'll look at a bit later.

You might notice that, frequently, the outside linebacker who plays opposite the tight end will line up right on the line with the defensive down linemen, so he can block the tight end on running plays or slow him down as he leaves on his pass route.

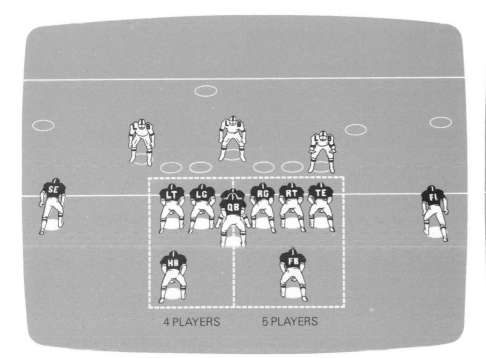

4 PLAYERS   5 PLAYERS

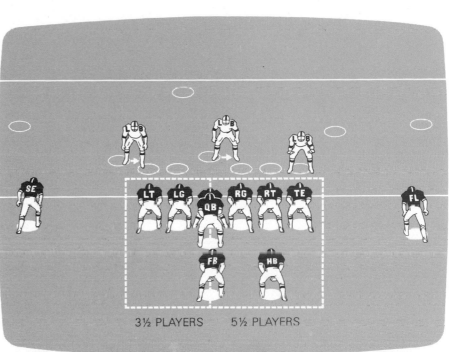

3½ PLAYERS   5½ PLAYERS

■ RUNNING STRENGTH

When the offense sets in its formation for the start of the play, linebackers key on the formation to determine the relative running strengths of each side of the formation. They do this by counting the offensive personnel.

Our example of the Open Set shows how this counting works. An imaginary line is drawn through the middle of the formation, cutting in half the center and the quarterback. The offensive men on each side of this line are then totaled,

counting the center and quarterback each as one-half man, and excluding the wide receivers.

In this Open Set formation, there are five players on the tight end side of this line and four players on the other side. The running strength in this formation therefore favors the tight end side by a factor of five to four. This is the 'normal' degree to which the tight end strengthens his side of the formation for running plays.

■ SHADING (STRONG SIDE SET)

Now let's look at how this running strength key affects the defense when the offense lines up in a Strong Side Set. With the two running backs shifted to the tight end side, there are five-and-a-half players on the side of the tight end (center ½, quarterback ½, right guard, right tackle, tight end, fullback ½, half-back), and three-and-a-half players on the other side.

The linebackers know that this formation favors the tight end side on running plays by a factor of 5½ to 3½.

To adjust for this bias, the line-backers will 'shade' from their normal defensive positions. The weak side outside linebacker and the middle linebacker will each move one-half a gap to the strong side. This shading puts them in better positions to defend against a run to the strong side.

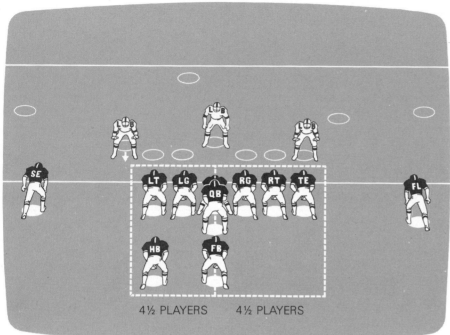

4 ½ PLAYERS   4 ½ PLAYERS

■ SHADING (WEAK SIDE SET)

If the offense lines up in a Weak Side Set, the running strength becomes balanced. There are four-and-a-half players on each side of the formation.

The linebackers will adjust for this balance by having the weak side linebacker move up and play right on the line. This puts him in slightly better position to defend against a run to the weak side.

The linebackers will vary the way they shade in response to different formations as they evaluate the running strength before each play. Understanding this 'running strength' key will help you to follow the shifting defensive positions of the linebackers and also confirm some of the predictions we made in the First Quarter about the types of plays run out of different formations.

■ LINE TO NEAREST BACK (STRONG SIDE SET)

Once the play starts, the linebackers must read whether the play is going to be a run or a pass. To do this, they key first on the offensive linemen in front of them to see whether they move forward (running play straight ahead), to either side (run to that side), or drop back (passing play). These are the same keys the defensive linemen feel for; the linebackers can actually look for this movement and react accordingly.

Additionally, the linebackers key on the movement of the running back nearest them. This key can reinforce the linebackers' initial read as to the type and direction of the play. In the Strong Side Set, illustrated here, the weak side linebacker keys through the left tackle and guard to the fullback, the middle linebacker keys through the center and quarterback to the fullback, and the strong side linebacker keys through the tight end to the halfback.

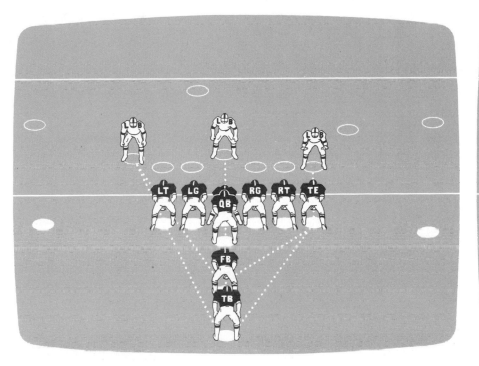

■ LINE TO RUNNING BACKS (I FORMATION)

When the offense is in an I Formation, there is no 'nearest' back, as both running backs are lined up directly behind the quarterback. In this case, all three linebackers must key through the offensive line to the quarterback and running backs as a unit in order to read the type and direction of the play.

This key underscores what we said in the First Quarter about the strength of the I Formation for running plays. Not only does it give the offense great flexibility in directing the play up the middle or to either side, but as we can see, the position of the running backs in this formation creates a more confusing key for the linebackers, with greater possibilities for deception by the offense.

■ OVERLOAD

We will be looking at pass defense in great detail later on, but let's look now at one important key for the middle linebacker when he plays man-for-man pass coverage. This is the 'second back out', or 'overload', key.

On standard man-for-man pass defense, the outside linebackers are each responsible for covering the running backs nearest them. If both backs run pass routes to either side, the middle linebacker is free to help out where needed.

If, however, both backs run pass routes to the same side of the field, trying to 'overload' the defense, the middle linebacker is responsible for covering the 'second' back to run a pass route to either side.

On passing plays (in man-for-man coverage), the outside linebackers will therefore key the nearest back to them, and the middle linebacker will key both running backs to read a possible overload.

Gap Responsibility

By now we are familiar with the ten potential running holes attacked by the offense and we know that these holes must be closed by the combined efforts of the defensive linemen and linebackers. Later we will see the schemes used by the four secondary defensive backs to help out on running plays, but for now let's look at some common schemes used by the linemen and linebackers to jam up these running holes or gaps. These schemes have been decided upon in advance by the defense and depend on the defensive alignment and the direction of the offensive play.

■ 4-3 DEFENSE VS. STRONG SIDE RUN

If the offense runs a play to the strong side and the defense is aligned in a 4-3 alignment, this is a standard scheme for closing seven of the ten potential running holes. The defensive tackles take the number zero and one holes and the defensive ends the four and five holes. The linebackers cover holes two, three, and six. These responsibilities were decided in advance in the defensive huddle. Notice that the defensive linemen are using their free arms to constrict the running holes and the linebackers come in to cover any open gaps. Even if this offensive play is a fake to the right and ends up coming inside or back to the left, seven of the running lanes are still covered.

Later we will see that the remaining holes are covered by the defensive secondary.

■ 4–3 DEFENSE
VS. WEAK SIDE RUN

Now look at how the assignments of the defensive linemen and linebackers change if the offense starts to run a play to the weak side. This is a variation of the strong side run responsibilities. In each case, the linebacker on the side of the field to which the play is being run has the outside gap, while the defensive end on the opposite side trails the play to guard against a reverse.

Both these examples show 'gap' blocking by the defense, in which each defender is responsible for one full gap to either side of an offensive man. The alternative to this is 'man' blocking by the defense, in which each defender is responsible for an offensive man and one-half a gap to each side of him.

■ 3–4 DEFENSE
VS. STRONG SIDE RUN

When the defense is aligned in a 3–4, the defensive linemen and linebackers have to change their gap responsibilities so that all running holes are plugged. This gap scheme is similar to the 4–3 Defense against a strong side run, except that the nose guard takes responsibility for an inside hole while the two inside linebackers provide backup.

You can see that the 3–4 Defense puts a bit less pressure right at the line, but gives a little more protection should the running play turn the corner past the first line of defense.

Stunts and Dogs

'Stunts' and 'dogs' are schemes used by the defensive linemen and linebackers to confuse the offense or to get a better angle of attack when a certain type of offensive play is expected. As we'll see, the defensive linemen and linebackers change from the usual gap responsibility we just finished watching. When the defensive linemen perform such tricks it is called 'stunting'; when the linebackers get involved it is called 'dogging'. All stunts and dogs are determined in the defensive huddle before the start of the play.

These stunts and dogs are counterparts to the trick offensive blocking schemes we watched in the First Quarter. Once you've learned these basic schemes, look for them on running plays that appear to be spectacularly successful or stopped cold. This is one aspect of the game where TV spectators have an edge, as stunts and dogs often appear clearly on the instant replay if the camera angle is from the end zone.

■ CROSS

On this stunt, two defensive linemen exchange defensive blocking assignments rather than charging straight ahead, as illustrated here by the defensive tackle and end. Such a move often confuses the offensive linemen if they are expecting the usual straight ahead defensive rush. If such a stunt is used on passing plays, the defensive linemen might have an easier time getting by the offensive pass protection and at the quarterback.

■ SCRAPE

This is a 'dog', since a linebacker is involved. The middle linebacker 'scrapes' around the outside of his strong side defensive tackle and into the offense's backfield, while the strong side defensive tackle also attacks forward. This dog puts pressure on the offensive line quicker than the normal defensive pattern we watched earlier, and can be effective in stopping a run or breaking up pass protection.

■ PLUG

This is a dog with two linebackers involved, shown here in a 3-4 defensive alignment. The two inside linebackers rush in along with the nose guard to 'plug' up an inside area. You'll see this dog used when the defense anticipates the direction of a running play. The plug is designed to add extra pressure to the area where the run is expected.

■ BLITZ

Although all linebacker dogs are sometimes called 'blitzes', usually this term is reserved for an out-and-out pass rush by one or more linebackers (or secondary men). In our illustration, the two outside linebackers in a 3-4 alignment are charging at the quarterback at the snap of the ball, in hopes of sacking him or at least pressuring him into a bad pass.

The liability with the blitz is that it removes one or more linebackers from being able to cover receivers or zones on passing plays. We'll look at pass coverage in detail when we watch the secondary.

Incidentally, it is common for one of the linebackers to rush the quarterback on every play when a 3-4 Defense is being used, regardless of whether a blitz is called.

■ PINCH

These next two stunts involve a coordinated scheme by all members of the defensive line. On the 'pinch', the defensive tackles and ends charge at an angle toward the center of the line. They'll try this stunt when a run up the middle is expected, and hope to throw the offensive linemen off their blocking pattern.

The outside gaps that are left open with this stunt must be covered by the linebackers.

■ SLANT

On this defensive line stunt, each of the defensive tackles and ends tries to squeeze through the offensive line at an angle, 'slanting' to one side. This stunt can be particularly effective if the defense has correctly anticipated an outside run. Once again, the vacated holes must be covered by the linebackers.

Tackling

So far we have seen the defensive linemen and linebackers protect against offensive blocks, key, plug gaps, stunt, and patrol their areas, all in an effort to get to the ball carrier. Now, if a ball carrier gets near them, they have to bring him to his knees in order to end the play. Their goal is to tackle the ball carrier or stack him up by stopping his forward progress.

Just as the defensive linemen and linebackers have techniques for rushing and stunting, they also have techniques for tackling. We are going to watch these tackling techniques during the next series of plays. As a general rule, the defender will watch and aim his tackling attack at the runner's midsection. The running back may be able to fake a defender with his head, shoulders, and legs, but he can't go in the opposite direction from his belt buckle.

■ SHOULDER TACKLE

The shoulder tackle is the most basic of all tackles. Notice that it starts much like the shoulder block. The defensive man moves in with his arms open, drops his body to the runner's belt, and drives his shoulder into his numbers. The defensive man then closes his arms around the ball carrier's legs, clasps his hands, lifts, and tries to throw him back and to the ground.

The rules state that only the ball carrier (or a faking ball carrier) can be tackled. If a running back is faking as if he has the ball, the defensive lineman will tackle him rather than assume it is a fake.

■ CROSS TACKLE

When a defensive man is coming at the ball carrier from the side and has enough time to get his body in front of the ball carrier, he uses a cross tackle. With his head and chest facing the runner's thighs, the defender throws his head and body in front of the ball carrier, locks his arms around his waist, and drives through him to stop his forward progress.

■ GANG TACKLE

It often takes more than one player to stop an especially powerful running back, and you'll frequently see two (or more) players 'ganging' up on the ball carrier. The first tackler to reach the ball carrier will aim his attack at the runner's midsection to slow his progress. Then additional tacklers will try to take him off his feet. If the first tackler aimed for the feet, he would run the risk of the ball carrier stepping out of the tackle and proceeding down the field.

■ TRIPPING UP

Although we will not be watching one of the more classic tackles when we see a defender who is lying on the ground reach out his hand and try to trip a runner, it is frequently used as a last-ditch effort to stop a ball carrier. Even though a defender has been blocked to the ground, he still must continue to do anything possible to detain or stop the offensive play. It is against the rules, however, for a defender to trip a ball carrier with his feet.

■ STRIPPING THE FOOTBALL

One tackling technique that you will surely see during the game is called 'stripping' the football, or trying to tackle the football. Not only do defenders attempt to bring the ball carrier down, but they also try to knock the football loose from the running back's possession, in the hopes of causing a fumble. The most usual technique for stripping the football is to pull at the arm of the ball carrier. This can be accomplished especially on a gang tackle. One defender can concentrate exclusively on stripping the running back of the football while the other brings him down.

The Secondary

Next we're going to watch the defensive secondary—the cornerbacks and safeties, who are also referred to as 'defensive backs'. The secondary men live and die by two rules: they always must assume that the offensive play is going to be a pass, and they must never let a potential receiver get behind them. Their primary job is, at worst, to prevent pass completions and, at best, to intercept passes.

All running plays also must be protected by these defensive backs, however, and so we are also going to watch how they set up schemes to pursue the ball carrier on running plays.

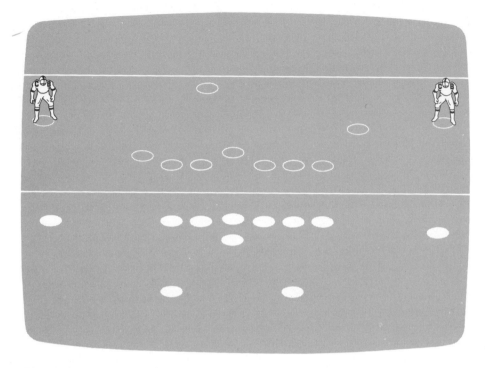

■ THE CORNERBACKS

The cornerbacks are the defensive men who play closest to the sidelines. They generally line up opposite the two offensive wide receivers, six or seven yards from them. (If the flanker moves over to the split end side in a slot position, his opposing cornerback usually will move over with him.)

The main job of the cornerbacks is to keep the wide receivers from catching passes, so they have to be as fast and agile as the receivers, while being strong enough to tackle them, should a pass be completed.

As we will see, the cornerbacks try to prevent pass receptions with a number of pass receiver coverage techniques, and various types of pass defenses. But the cornerbacks don't work only on passing plays. On running plays, the cornerbacks work with the defensive linemen, linebackers, and the safeties in a coordinated pursuit of the ball carrier.

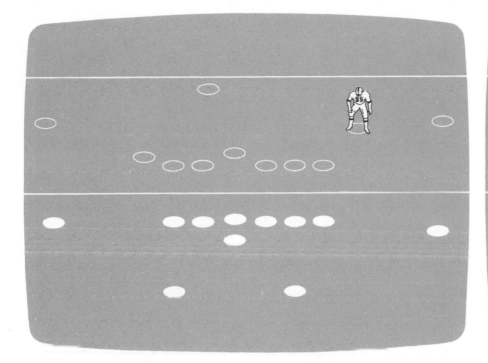

■ THE STRONG SAFETY

The strong safety lines up a bit behind the linebackers on the strong side of the field, usually outside the tight end. Both the cornerbacks and the safeties use an upright stance similar to the linebackers.

The strong safety is usually responsible for a running lane on running plays and for being part of the pass defense on passing plays. Because he is closer to the quarterback than other members of the secondary, he also can be assigned to give up his area and rush the quarterback with a 'strong safety blitz'.

Like the cornerbacks, the strong safety must be quick and agile, but the strong safety has to be more physical, since he frequently is called upon to make tackles on running plays. His job calls for flexibility in dealing with blocking, running, and passing defense, much like the tight end's job on the offensive team.

■ THE FREE SAFETY

The job of the free safety is almost exclusively pass defense. He is the deepest defender on the defensive unit, usually playing slightly to the weak side of the defensive backfield. All of the secondary men will vary the depth and lateral position that they play in the defensive backfield according to the offensive formation and their guess as to the offensive play.

The free safety is often the last resort for stopping receivers who have eluded their pass defenders. His general assignment on pass plays is therefore to be deeper than the deepest offensive receiver. Occasionally, however, the free safety will rush the quarterback with a 'free safety blitz'. The free safety must have great speed to cover a large area of the field; he is much like the center fielder in baseball.

Secondary Keys

We saw that the defensive linemen and linebackers looked for keys, or clues, to give them an advantage in determining or reacting to the offensive play. The secondary men also key the offense to gain whatever advantage they can in trying to stop the offensive drive. Some of these keys can be made before the play begins; others come as the play is in progress.

These keys are useful to us as spectators, too, if we want to anticipate the play. We'll now take a look at some of the keys that are most reliable in helping the defensive secondary. (The linebackers also look for these keys to help them react to passing situations.) Remember, though, that keying is a tricky business. It involves much guesswork, and the offense may try the unexpected.

■ **OFFENSIVE FORMATION**

Since the secondary is primarily concerned with pass coverage, one of their most important keys is the offensive formation. We saw in the last quarter that certain offensive formations favor running or passing attacks. The Open Set formation is usually a passing formation. The Single Set Back is an almost sure passing situation. These formations provide keys to the secondary that they will lead to passing plays.

Our example shows the flanker going in motion to a slot formation, next to the split end—another likely passing situation. In this case, the strong side cornerback will usually move across the field so that he can play opposite the flanker, as this is the man he usually covers on man-for-man pass defense. (If the tight end were to move over wide to the strong side, the strong safety's usual move would be to shade over with him.)

■ RECEIVER TENDENCIES

The cornerbacks and safeties key on receiver tendencies to get a jump on the pass. By studying past game films, they often spot quirks that signal what the receivers will be doing. A receiver might start his pattern by racing downfield when he is really going to stop for a medium pass, cut to the outside before running to the inside, or tend to run a particular pattern in certain field position situations.

■ QUARTERBACK DROP

The quarterback drop is somewhat of a key to the distance of the pass. If the quarterback takes only a few steps and prepares to throw, it should be a short pass; if he drops back seven or nine yards, it could be a bomb.

The cornerbacks and safeties also know that the quarterback can't throw an accurate pass to any area of the field unless he is looking there. The head of the quarterback is therefore some clue as to where the pass is going.

■ OFFENSIVE LINEMEN

It is against the rules of the game for any offensive lineman to move forward of the line of scrimmage on a passing play until the ball is thrown. This rule is useful to the cornerbacks and safeties, as they can key on the offensive linemen and know that the play is a run if any of those linemen move toward them. Then they can forget about the pass and move forward to help the rest of the defense stop the running play.

■ RUNNING BACKS

Once a running back runs past the line of scrimmage with the ball, a pass cannot be thrown. The secondary can then move in and help stop the running play. The secondary has to be careful, though; a fake handoff might deceive them into thinking a ball carrier has crossed the line while the quarterback still has the ball and is preparing to pass. This is why "Always think pass" is the basic rule of the secondary.

Receiver Coverage

Soon we will see that pass defense involves the defensive secondary and linebackers either covering the receivers on a man-for-man basis, covering the field with various zone defenses, or using a combination of both man-for-man and zone coverage to make sure no receiver is wide open. But, even though a receiver is theoretically covered, it doesn't necessarily mean he can't come up with a pass reception. To counteract the pass catching skills and techniques of the offensive receivers we watched in the First Quarter, the defensive backs have developed pass coverage techniques of their own. We'll watch for some of them on the next few passing plays.

■ JAMMING

The defense is allowed to 'jam', or 'chuck', meaning to give an eligible receiver one block, push, or shove within five yards of the line of scrimmage. Once a receiver has passed five yards over the line of scrimmage he can't be touched by a defender unless the receiver has caught the ball or both he and the defender are going for the pass at the same time.

The defender (usually a cornerback) uses the legal chuck to throw the receiver off balance or detain him from running his pass pattern. The defender uses his hands and not his shoulder or body because he must stay afoot so he can still defend against the pass.

This technique can give the defensive man an edge on the speedy receiver, especially if he can force the receiver to run a route different from the one he was assigned. It is also used to give the jamming cornerback's teammates time to get to their assigned areas of the field on zone pass coverage.

■ PLAYING THE MAN

On man-for-man pass coverage, it is important that the pass defender watch his man and not look for the ball until the receiver reaches up his hands to catch it. The defender knows the receiver can't run his pattern properly with his hands up in the air. The defender watches the receiver's belt buckle so he won't be fooled by a head fake. Once the defender sees the receiver's arms go up, he can expect that the ball is on the way. At that point he looks for the football and leaps to bat it down or intercept it.

As we'll see in the next section, whether the defensive backs (especially the cornerbacks) try to keep the receiver to the inside or outside depends in part on the type of pass defense being employed by the secondary.

■ PLAYING THE BALL

Once the defender sees the ball coming toward a receiver, he can choose either to bat it to the ground, forcing an incompletion, or to take a stab at intercepting the football. The defender will put one hand between the receiver's hands, while keeping the other arm free to make a tackle in case the receiver catches the pass.

It is always safer to bat the ball away from the receiver rather than trying to intercept it. If the defender goes for an interception he can mistime his grab, allowing the ball to be caught by the receiver, or bat the ball in the air, allowing one of the receivers another shot at a pass completion.

If all else fails, the defender can try to tackle the receiver at the instant he catches the ball, jarring the ball loose. This is called 'timing the hit', and is legal.

Pass Defense

The quarterback drops back, cocks his arm, and gets ready to throw. This is the critical moment when the secondary and the linebackers have to make sure that every potential pass receiver is covered. If you're attending the game, you will see that pass defense demands teamwork and discipline. Occasionally, we get to see the whole picture on TV, but unfortunately, most of the time the camera zeros in on the quarterback and the ball sailing through the air, and on the instant replay we rarely get to see the individual pass route run by the receiver. Whether you're a season ticket holder or glued to the tube, however, you'll appreciate the passing game much more if you learn to look for these pass defense systems.

■ MAN-FOR-MAN

The most basic type of pass coverage is 'man-for-man'. The diagram shows one possible set of man-for-man assignments. The two cornerbacks are responsible for the wide receivers, while the strong safety covers the tight end. The two outside linebackers each take the nearest running back. These assignments match offensive and defensive players with the same physical abilities.

The middle linebacker is the 'overload' man. On a passing play, he is responsible for covering the second running back to come out of the backfield to either side. If the running backs run pass routes to each side of the field, the middle linebacker is free to help where needed in the 'underneath' area about ten yards past the line of scrimmage.

The free safety is the free man in the 'deep' area of the defensive backfield. He is available to pick up any receiver who eludes the other defenders.

■ MAN—DOUBLE COVERAGE

This is a variation on the man-for-man pass coverage we just looked at. The only change is that the free safety and weak side cornerback are double-teaming the split end. This often happens when the split end is so fast and tricky that it is too difficult for one man to cover him. The cornerback can try to stay in front of the split end while the free safety covers him from behind. The cornerback and free safety can also double-team the split end with one defensive back protecting the inside area (toward the center of the field) and the other protecting the outside.

Notice that the middle linebacker is still an overload man; that is, he must cover man-for-man the second running back out of the backfield to either side, or play free in the underneath area if the backs run to opposite sides of the field.

■ DOUBLE-DOUBLE COVERAGE

We just saw an example of double coverage, with the free safety and weak side cornerback double-teaming the split end. It also may be necessary for the defenders to put man-for-man double coverage on the flanker. In our example, the flanker is double-teamed by the strong side cornerback and the strong safety. The middle linebacker now covers the fullback while the strong side linebacker covers the tight end. (The strong side and middle linebackers might switch men if the fullback runs a pattern to the strong side.)

This coverage could be a response to the threat of a long pass or particularly talented receivers. Notice that there are no longer any overload or free defenders.

Even when the pass defense is man-for-man, the defenders work as a team. The key to pass defense is knowing where your help is.

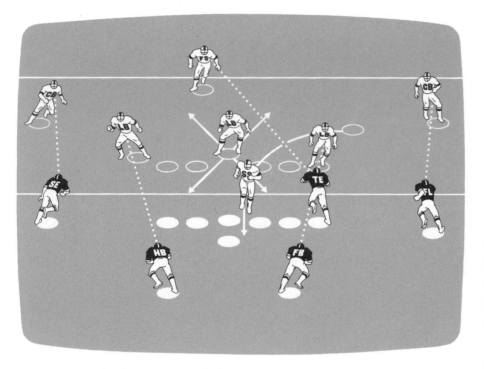

■ STRONG SAFETY BLITZ

This is another variation of man-for-man pass defense. In this situation, the strong safety will attack between the center and offensive right tackle as soon as the quarterback starts his pass drop.

The free safety must then pick up the strong safety's man and play man-for-man coverage on the tight end on this play. At the snap of the ball, the free safety will shift, moving over and in to be able to cover the tight end. If he made his move before the snap, the quarterback might be able to 'read' the blitz and change the play to adjust for it.

Generally, on the strong safety blitz, you will also see one or two linebackers blitz. No matter how many defenders blitz, the remaining linebackers and defensive backs will play man-for-man coverage.

■ ZONE DEFENSE— STRONG ROTATION, CORNERBACK ZONE

In theory, man-for-man defense looks like it should work just fine. The problem is that the receivers know where they are going and therefore always have an edge over the defenders assigned to cover them. For this reason, you'll frequently see the defense use a form of 'zone' defense.

Here's an example of a common seven-zone pass defense, out of a 4–3 alignment. First, look at how the defensive side of the field is divided into seven zones. There are four 'underneath' zones: two 'flat' zones, one at each side of the field, and two 'curl' zones in the middle. (The area at the center of the underneath part of the field is sometimes called the 'hook' area.) The defensive backfield is divided into three 'deep' zones: two 'deep outside' zones and a 'deep middle' zone.

In this particular seven-zone defense, the linebackers and defensive backs cover the zones as follows:
- The weak side linebacker covers the weak side flat zone.
- The middle linebacker covers the weak side curl zone.
- The strong side linebacker covers the strong side curl zone.
- The strong side cornerback covers the strong side flat zone.
- The weak side cornerback covers the weak side deep zone.
- The free safety covers the middle deep zone.
- The strong safety covers the strong side deep zone.

Zone defenses are identified in a number of ways. First, this would be called a 'four under/three deep' zone defense to distinguish the number of zones closest to the line of scrimmage and deep in the defensive backfield. This would also be called a 'strong rotation' zone defense. If you imagine all the defenders as the spokes of a wheel, you can see that the backfield part of the wheel is 'rotating' to the strong side of the field. Finally, this would be called a 'cornerback' zone defense, indicating that in this pass defense, the cornerback covers the strong side flat zone. (A zone defense in which the cornerback covers the strong flat zone is also sometimes called a 'cloud' zone, the word 'cloud' having the same first letter as 'cornerback'.)

All of these terms may seem a bit confusing at first, but it will be easier to remember the different types of zone pass coverage if you learn some of these basic concepts. Also, before we move on, make sure that you're thoroughly familiar with the 'strong side/weak side' terminology we looked at in the beginning of the First Quarter. We'll be using these terms for the rest of this section on defense, and throughout the Third Quarter when we watch plays.

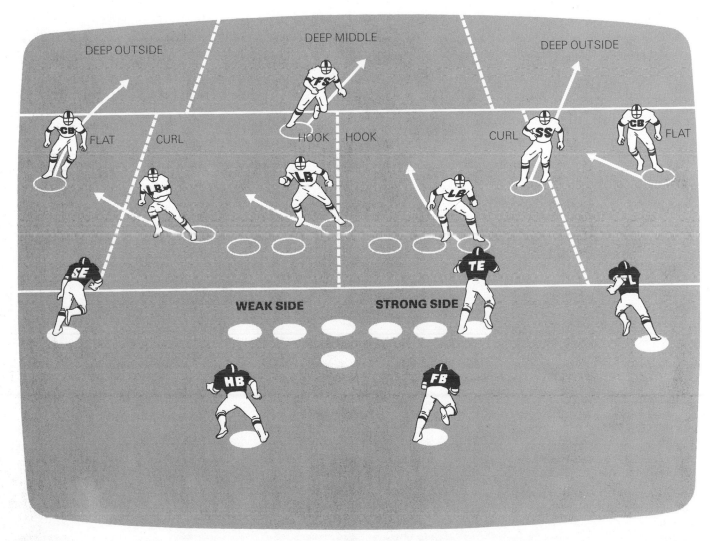

■ STRONG SAFETY ZONE

In the 'strong safety' zone defense, the strong safety covers the strong flat zone while the cornerback takes the strong deep zone. This is also called a 'sky' zone ('sky' = 'strong safety'). It is also called an 'inverted' zone defense, since the cornerback and strong safety are inverting the normal cornerback zone assignments illustrated in the previous example. (The rotation is still to the strong side.)

The inversion of the cornerback and strong safety assignments could confuse the flanker, as he might not be sure who is covering him, or whether he is facing man-for-man or zone coverage.

The basic rule of zone pass defense is "Play as deep as the deepest man in your zone." For this reason, zone defenses tend to 'concede' short passes while guarding more against long completions. Even so, the zone defenders stay aware of how the passing play is proceeding and where the other defenders are.

■ WEAK ROTATION ZONE

Here's what it looks like when the defense rotates to the weak side. The pass defense is rotating counter-clockwise, or toward the weak side of the offensive formation. Here the strong side linebacker takes the strong flat zone.

While zone coverage assigns responsibilities for particular areas of the field, keep in mind that all defenders work together. For example, in this weak rotation, the strong side cornerback, outside linebacker, and middle linebacker work as a unit to defend the strong side of the field.

■ FOUR-DEEP ZONE

In the cloud and sky zone defenses there were four underneath, or 'short', zones and three deep, or 'long', zones. The 'four-deep' zone defense parcels off the field to create three short and four long zones.

This zone defense anticipates a long pass. It reduces the possibility of two receivers coming into the same zone, or 'flooding' the zone in the deep area, although the underneath area is left slightly undermanned. You might see this defense at the end of the game when the losing offensive team needs a long pass.

The cornerbacks will usually try to keep the wide receivers to the inside on zone coverage. This is because it is important for the defenders to see the quarterback throw the ball in zone defense, and by staying to the outside, the defender can keep an eye on both the quarterback and the receiver.

■ FIVE UNDER/TWO DEEP ZONE

This is a zone defense that would be used when a short pass is expected. The underneath area is divided into five zones, covered in this example by the linebackers and cornerbacks. The two deep zones are covered by the free safety and strong safety. Any receiver trying to pick up a few yards on a quick pass will likely find a defender waiting for him.

The defense will continually alternate among various man-for-man and zone defenses to keep the offense guessing. Seasoned quarterbacks are proficient at reading the defensive pass coverage as they drop back to pass. The more pass defense variety the defense throws at the quarterback, the less chance he will have to pick out his prime receivers.

FIVE UNDER MAN/ TWO DEEP ZONE

This is one example of a 'combination' pass defense that is part zone and part man-for-man. All five of the receivers are covered on a man-for-man basis by the cornerbacks and linebackers, while the strong safety and free safety drop back to cover the deep area in two zones.

This defense is an attempt to have the benefits of both types of pass defense. Each receiver will be pressured man-for-man, with the safeties as backup in case a receiver breaks away.

There are other types of combination man/zone defenses possible — for example, playing man-for-man in the middle of the field and zone along the sidelines.

STRONG SAFETY ZONE (3-4 DEFENSE)

We'll end by looking at a few pass defenses run out of a 3-4 alignment. Our example of the strong safety, or sky, zone illustrates how the additional linebacker is used on many passing plays. Here, the weak inside linebacker rushes the quarterback. When in the 3-4 alignment, the defense will rush with different linebackers throughout the game to keep the offense confused. This added element

of surprise is another edge that many feel the 3-4 Defense gives over the passing game.

If one or both running backs do not go out to run pass routes, but stay back to protect the quarterback, one or two linebackers will usually rush. Not only is extra pass rushing pressure needed to counteract the extra pass protection, but the defense knows that it will have one or two less receivers to cover.

■ FIVE UNDER/THREE DEEP ZONE (3–4 DEFENSE)

This is one zone defense that is possible only out of the 3–4 Defense. All four linebackers and the four secondary men drop back to provide maximum zone coverage. This guards very effectively against any length pass.

Eight pass defenders could also be used in a five under man/three deep zone coverage, similar to the combination coverage we looked at previously.

■ MAN-FOR-MAN—FREE SAFETY AND LINEBACKER BLITZ (3–4 DEFENSE)

Our final example shows man-for-man coverage out of a 3–4 Defense, with the free safety, as well as two linebackers, blitzing the quarterback. Since the free safety is primarily responsible for protecting against a long pass, his blitz is usually a shocker to the offense. To add to the shock, the defense often will commit several defenders to the blitz.

When this type of blitz is used, it is a gamble. The decision has been made to try for a sack, at the expense of weakening the pass defense.

Run Pursuit

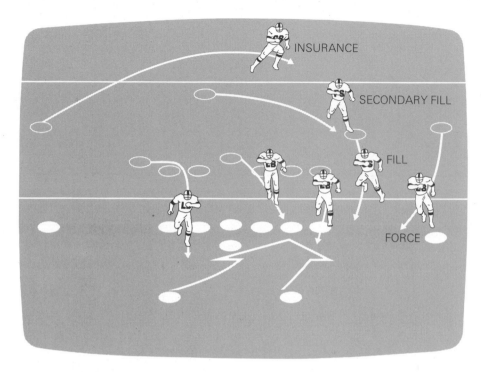

We already have seen some secondary keys that tell the defensive backs when the play is a running play. Once the secondary knows the play is a run it must attack to help the defensive linemen and linebackers stop the ball carrier.

On running plays the four defensive backs have one of four jobs. One defensive back is responsible for 'force', or 'containment': keeping the run to the inside by attacking the play from outside in. A second defensive back is responsible for 'fill': plugging the hole at the spot on the field where the run is being aimed. The third defensive back provides 'secondary fill' by shading toward the hole where the run is being aimed. Finally, the fourth defensive back is responsible for 'insurance'; he must get to the side of the field where the run is being aimed and stay deep enough to make a tackle if the ball carrier breaks loose past all the other defenders.

■ 4–3 DEFENSE VS. STRONG SIDE RUN

Earlier we saw an example of the defensive line and linebacker responsibilities if they are in a 4–3 alignment and the offense runs a play to the strong side. In this example we can see the linebackers carrying out their assignments as we saw earlier. Now look at the four defensive backs. The strong side cornerback comes in to 'force' or 'contain' the play to the inside. The strong safety is responsible for 'fill' by coming in to cover the wide number eight hole. The free safety also converges on this area as 'secondary fill' for the running hole. The weak side cornerback cuts across the field and keeps deep to act as 'insurance' in case the runner breaks loose. Incidentally, once the weak side linebacker is sure the run is away from his side, he should attack at least as deep as the ball carrier and pursue him in case of an opposite field run.

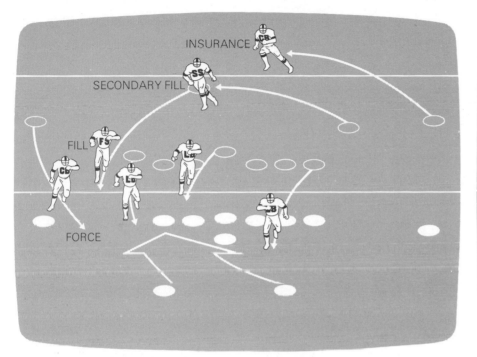

INSURANCE

SECONDARY FILL

FILL

FORCE

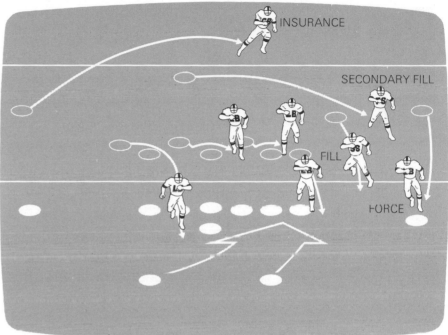

INSURANCE

SECONDARY FILL

FILL

FORCE

■ 4–3 DEFENSE VS. WEAK SIDE RUN

On this running play to the weak side, the four defensive backs use a different scheme to perform their four functions. This time the weak side cornerback comes over to force or contain the play, while the free safety fills the wide hole. The strong safety comes across the field to act as secondary fill and the strong side cornerback follows the run and stays deep in case the ball carrier breaks loose.

These responsibilities depend on the pass defense scheme that has been called in the defensive huddle. For example, if the weak side cornerback's pass defense assignment were to cover the weak deep zone, the weak side linebacker would have force responsibility.

■ 3–4 DEFENSE VS. STRONG SIDE RUN

The run pursuit assignments are basically the same out of the 3–4 defensive alignment. Against a strong side run, the strong side cornerback provides force; the strong safety, fill; and the free safety and weak side cornerback, secondary fill and insurance. The strong inside linebacker is also available here to provide, in effect, additional fill.

Defensive Alignment Variations

In one sense, the defensive alignment varies on every play. We have already seen that the defense does not have to stay set before the play begins, and that they continually shift as the quarterback is calling his signals, to get in the best position to defend the play. The linebackers will shift or shade to the strong or weak side, depending on the formation of the running backs, and will shift up to the line or back, depending on whether the formation and the game situation indicate a probable run or pass. The secondary men will move across the field to follow their man assignments, and will also move up or back to anticipate long or short passes.

The variations that we are going to look at now are of a different type. They all involve substituting defensive players so that the defensive personnel will be better adapted to the game situation.

■ **SITUATIONS AND PERSONNEL**

The key to these situation alignments is that the defensive personnel itself changes. When the defense must align itself to protect against a run it will add down lineman players. When it anticipates a pass it will use a preponderance of defensive backs.

Keep track of which players the defense is using for its 'standard' defense (usually a 4-3 or 3-4). While the offense is in its huddle, watch the defensive huddle to see whether and where the defense is making substitutions. These changes can let you know what the defense is thinking, and provide you with additional keys to the next play.

Generally, these defensive variations can be thought of in terms of 'line personnel variations'—those that add down linemen—and 'backfield personnel variations'—those that add secondary men (defensive backs).

Line Personnel Variations

You will remember from watching the defensive line at the beginning of this quarter that down linemen are strong, big, tough blockers that are hard to run through. Usually you see three or four down linemen in on a play because the defense wants to have the flexibility to protect against both a run or a pass. But, as the probability of a run increases, you will see more down linemen come into the game and line up in a three- or four-point stance. You will see the maximum number of down linemen on a goal line defense or when the defense is going to rush to block a punt, field goal, or extra point.

■ 3-4 DEFENSE

This is one of the standard alignments we have been watching throughout this quarter. There are three down linemen and four linebackers.

This alignment (as well as the 4-3 Defense) makes use of what is called a 'seven-man front'—seven players filling the defensive line and linebacker positions. The seven-man front is virtually standard in professional football, where in most situations the defense must be prepared for both strong running and passing attacks.

Eight-man fronts (e.g., four defensive linemen and four linebackers) are sometimes seen in college and high school football, where the passing threat may not be as great.

■ 4-3 DEFENSE

This is our other standard alignment. There are four down linemen and three linebackers.

Throughout this quarter, we have seen that the difference between the 4-3 and the 3-4 Defenses is mainly one of personnel. The 4-3 Defense, with more linemen than linebackers, puts more pressure at the line to block against running plays and to pass rush on passing plays. The 3-4 Defense, with more linebackers than defensive linemen, provides somewhat better protection against passes and, to some degree, with regard to run pursuit.

■ FLEX DEFENSE

The 'flex' defense is a variation on the 4-3 Defense that is based on the notion of 'stunting', or linemen exchanging responsibilities.

Notice that the weak side defensive tackle and the strong side defensive end are not on the line of scrimmage, but instead are playing one-and-a-half to two yards back off the line of scrimmage. These 'flexed' positions give the linemen and linebackers more room to execute both normal gap blocking and the types of stunts and dogs we looked at earlier in this quarter. The constant threat of a change in gap assignment is designed to confuse the offensive line. The Flex Defense always employs gap defensive blocking as opposed to man blocking.

Although some professional teams have used the Flex Defense with apparent success, many coaches feel that the constant switching of assignments complicates the work of the defensive line.

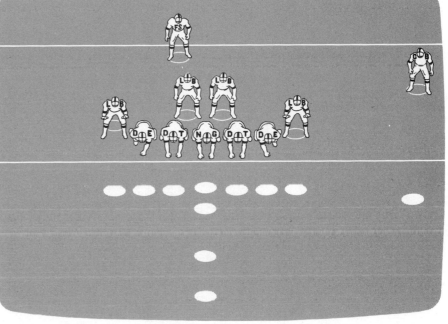

■ 5-2 DEFENSE

The 5-2 alignment is another seven-man-front defense; it puts five defensive linemen on the line, two linebackers behind them, and the usual four defensive backs in the secondary. This is a long-pass-protection alignment which gives the defense a strong five man pass rush while leaving four men in the secondary to cover the pass. Since the underneath linebacker area is only protected by two defenders, this alignment more or less concedes the short pass.

■ 5-4 DEFENSE

Here we have a short yardage situation where the defense thinks a run is likely, and the defense has responded with a nine-man-front defense. There are five down linemen: four lined up as in a 4-3 Defense, plus a nose guard. There are four linebackers playing as they would in a 3-4 Defense. To protect against a trick pass play, the defense keeps two men in the secondary.

This alignment gives maximum protection against a run or a short pass; usually you will see this used when the offense needs to pick up one or two yards for a first down. (Notice that the offense has 'confirmed' the defense's reading of the situation by lining up with two tight ends and the running backs in an I Formation.)

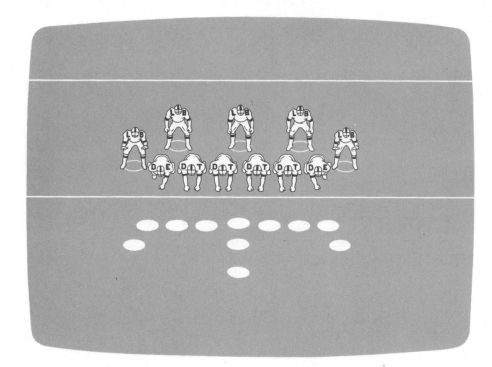

Backfield Personnel Variations

As the probability of a running play increases, the defense will put in more down linemen to stack up the run. But, as the chance of a pass play increases, these down linemen (and sometimes linebackers) are taken out and replaced by secondary defensive backs, who are better able to protect against the pass. Sometimes, when the situation calls for an almost sure pass, you will see as many as six or seven defensive backs taking up the positions of linebackers and the secondary.

■ 6–5 (GOAL LINE) DEFENSE

The surest running situation for the offense occurs when it is within a few yards of the defensive goal line with three or four downs to get in for a score. Since it is safer to run the ball than it is to pass it, the offense will be in a run situation, and this run more than likely will be aimed right up the middle.

The defense now has lined up in a 6–5 'Goal Line' Defense to protect its end zone. There are six down linemen opposite the offensive line, backed up by five linebacker players. All eleven defenders will be close to the line of scrimmage, both because a run is expected and also because there is so little area to protect against the pass. This is one of the toughest assignments the defense faces. (Notice that the offense is in a double wing formation for its goal line plunge.)

■ NICKEL DEFENSE (3 DEFENSIVE LINEMEN)

The 'Nickel' Defense gets its name because there are five defensive backs in this defense. It is used when the offense is expected to pass. All five men in the defensive secondary will be defensive back players (cornerbacks and safeties) to protect against the pass.

The addition of the extra defensive back necessitates a 'six-man front', with three defensive linemen and three linebackers.

■ NICKEL DEFENSE (4 DEFENSIVE LINEMEN)

We have just shown the nickel defense being created by taking out a defensive lineman and adding a fifth defensive back. This provides good short and long pass protection, but a rather weak pass rush because there are only three down linemen.

Another way to protect against the long pass is to leave in four defensive linemen to rush while substituting a defensive back for a linebacker. This way of aligning the nickel defense weakens the underneath linebacker area and makes it vulnerable to the short pass, but strengthens protection against the long pass, not only because of the five defensive backs, but also because the four-linemen pass rush will reduce the time that the quarterback has available to throw.

■ DIME DEFENSE

The 'Dime' Defense takes the Nickel Defense one step further, by putting six defensive backs in the game. Both the wide receivers can be double-covered here. Such an alignment and personnel change sometimes occurs late in the game, when the offensive team is so far behind that the defense knows it must pass to catch up. The defense is willing to give up a short pass or run to guard against a bomb.

Any type of defense in which the main goal is to guard against a long pass is called a 'prevent' defense.

■ MONSTER DEFENSE

You will see this alignment in college football. Basically, this is a 3–4 alignment with one extra linebacker, who can alternate between being used as a linebacker or secondary man. He is called a 'monster' because the offense is not sure what he will do.

The monster's main job is to patrol the 'widest side' of the field — the side of

the field with the most area from where the ball is spotted to the sideline. (See a discussion of the 'hash marks' on the field in the Officials, Rules, and Penalties section.)

Special Teams: The Kicking Game

Now that we have covered all the offensive and defensive positions, we will end this Second Quarter by looking at the personnel on the 'special teams'.

The special teams are so-called because they are made up of players who come into the game to perform the unique assignments involved in the kicking game. These players generally are not the same players that you have watched on the offensive and defensive teams. Most football teams, especially professional teams, are not willing to let their first-string players put their bodies on the line to face the dangers of the special team assignments. So, the special team players usually are made up of second-string players and rookies.

This doesn't mean, however, that the kicking game is unimportant. In fact, it is well known in football that kicking is one-third of the game; about one-third of all points scored in football are a result of the kicking game. In fact, some head coaches consider the special teams so important that they are leaning toward using their first-string personnel for these assignments.

We'll take a look here at the special team formations and the types of players who make up each special team. The different types of kicking plays and the assignments of each of the players on those plays will be covered in the Third Quarter. There are six special teams or kicking situations: the kickoff, the kickoff return, the punt, the punt return, the field goal and extra-point try, and the field goal and extra-point defense. There are a variety of ways in which these teams can carry out their jobs, but our examples show standard situations that you are likely to see during a game.

The Kickoff

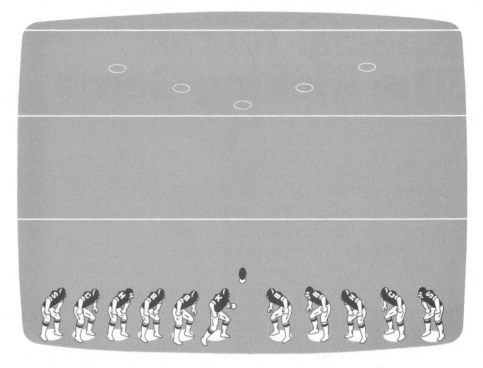

The kickoff starts the game, the second half, and over-time play in professional football. The ball is also kicked off after either team scores during the game. In a professional game, the ball is spotted for the kickoff on the 35-yard line nearest the kickoff team's goal (40-yard line in college and high school).

Because the opposing team will have possession of the ball once it is kicked, the kickoff team is made up primarily of defensive players who are accustomed to tackling and whose job it is to keep the kickoff return team from running the ball back.

■ THE KICKOFF FORMATION

The kickoff formation is made up of a 'placekicker' (K), two inside men on each side of the placekicker who are called 'wedge busters' (B), two men whose job is to tackle the ball carrier who are called 'head hunters' (H), two 'contain' men (C) to force the ball carrier toward the inside, and two 'safeties' (S) on the extreme ends of the formation.

The placekicker stands back a few yards from the ball so he can run to gain speed and momentum to help his kick. The other ten kickoff players are spread evenly across the field in a straight line, behind the football. They will watch the placekicker and move forward with him, but they must stay behind the football until it is kicked. Once the placekicker's foot touches the football, all eleven players move downfield to perform their individual assignments.

The Wedge Busters. The four players (two on each side of the place-kicker) at the inside of the kickoff formation are called wedge busters. When we look at the kickoff return team, we will see that it usually tries to return the kickoff by forming a wedge of blockers up the middle for the ball carrier. It is the job of these four inside men in the kickoff formation to bust this wedge and get at the ball carrier. These inside men must be mobile and tough. They must be willing to run full speed downfield and collide with the wedge blockers. Usually you will find offensive and defensive linemen and linebackers in these four positions.

The Head Hunters. Next to the wedge busters on each side of the formation are the head hunters, whose job is to get downfield and behind the wedge to tackle the ball carrier. To accomplish this, they need speed and the ability to tackle. Generally you will find linebackers playing these positions.

The Contain Men. Next to each head hunter on both sides of the kickoff formation are contain men. Their job is to get downfield quickly and contain the kickoff return by forcing the ball carrier toward their head-hunting and wedge-busting teammates, who are approaching from the middle. Since speed is needed to accomplish this, generally you will find running backs, wide receivers, and safeties filling these positions.

The Safeties. At the extreme ends of the kickoff formation, nearest each sideline, you will see the two safeties. The job of these men is to hang back and protect their sides of the field in case their teammates fail to stop the ball carrier and he breaks loose. Since great speed is required to do this job, you will see wide receivers and cornerbacks in these roles.

■ THE PLACEKICKER (TOE-STYLE)

The placekicker is a specialist; usually he comes into the game just for the kick-off and for the field goal and extra-point try. He gets his name because the ball is in place on the ground when he kicks it. (On the kickoff only, the ball may be placed on a kicking tee.)

The placekicker must kick deep for distance, so that the return team receives the ball close to its goal line, and for 'hang time'— the time the ball stays in the air—so that the kickoff team has time to get downfield to make a tackle.

Two kicking styles are now used in football. In the older, more traditional 'toe' kick, illustrated here, the kicker's foot meets the ball head-on. We'll see the 'soccer-style' kick when we look at the field goal and extra-point situation.

After he has kicked off, the place-kicker hangs back and guards the middle of the field in case the ball carrier breaks loose.

The Kickoff Return

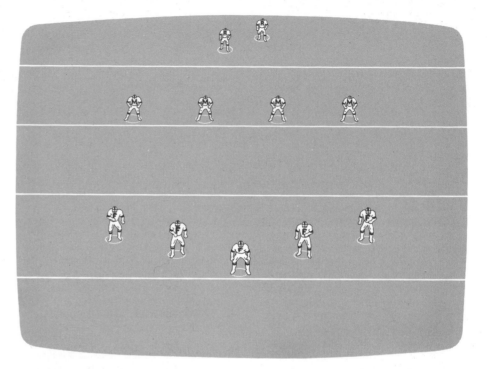

The kickoff return team wants to take the kickoff and bring the football as far back upfield as possible. It will do this either by forming a wall for the ball carrier along either sideline or by forming a wedge up the middle. The decision as to whether to form a wedge or a wall usually is based on whether the kickoff goes up the middle of the field or to either side.

    To accomplish this risky assignment, the kickoff return unit is made up of two fleet runners and nine tough blockers. Since the kickoff return is a ball-carrying situation, usually you will see offensive players in these roles, since they are used to blocking for the ball carrier.

■ **THE KICKOFF RETURN FORMATION**
    There are three layers of players in a standard kickoff return formation. First, there are five 'front men' (F), who block the charge of the kickoff team. Next, there are four 'middle men' (M), who block for the two 'return men' (R), who return the kick.

    The Front Men. The rules require that the kickoff return team line up no closer than ten yards from where the ball

is spotted for the kickoff. Usually you'll see the front men on the kicking team's 45-yard line. Their main job is to block by taking on the four 'wedge buster' inside men on the kickoff team. The five front men have to be big enough to block, yet still be mobile. Usually you will see guards, linebackers, and tight ends playing these front positions.

    The Middle Men. The second layer of players in the kickoff return formation consists of the four middle men. They line up about thirty yards behind the front men, on their own 25-yard line. Their job is to form the wedge for the ball carrier to help him upfield. Since they have to be tough blockers accustomed to blocking for the ball carrier, generally you will find offensive linemen — tackles, guards, and centers — playing these positions. Often, however, one of the four is a fullback type who can field the ball and run it if the kick is short, as well as perform the blocking assignment if the kick goes further downfield to the return men.

The Return Men. The two return men, who line up inside their own 10-yard line, are perhaps the most important specialty positions on the kickoff return team. They must be able to catch the football and run it as far back upfield as possible. Although there are specialists who play only this position, sometimes you will see wide receivers or lightning-fast running backs at this

position. (Some teams use only one player in the return man position; in that case, there is an additional blocker.)

On the kickoff, if the ball is kicked over the return team's goal line, or if a member of the return team catches the ball in his end zone and 'grounds' it by dropping to one knee, the ball is automatically spotted on the return team's 20-yard line, for the start of play. For this reason, the return man who catches the kickoff in the end zone must decide whether it is worth risking a run back and being tackled short of his 20-yard line.

Another consideration on the kickoff is the rule that permits any player on the kickoff team to recover the ball once it has gone at least ten yards beyond the kickoff spot position or has touched a return player. For this reason, the return man must catch the ball; he can't afford to let it bounce around on the field. This rule makes possible the 'onside kick', which is a purposely short kickoff that the kickoff team hopes to recover. We'll look at this play, and the more standard kickoff return plays, in the Third Quarter.

■ THE FAIR CATCH

If a return man chooses not to run back the football, he may raise one hand in the air while the ball is in flight, signaling a 'fair catch'. When he does this, it is illegal for any members of the kickoff team to touch him; they must let him catch the ball. The return man will fair catch when he knows he will be hit by an opposing player as soon as he catches the ball. In this case, it is safer to fair catch than to be hit and risk fumbling.

Just because a return man signals a fair catch, the ball is not automatically his; he must catch it. If he drops the ball, it is a fumble and anyone's ball. Once a return man has made a fair catch, he may not advance with the ball.

The rules permit calling for a fair catch on both a kickoff and a punt. As we'll see in the next section, 'hang time' is more of a factor in the punting situation, so this is where you'll see practically all fair catches called.

The Punt

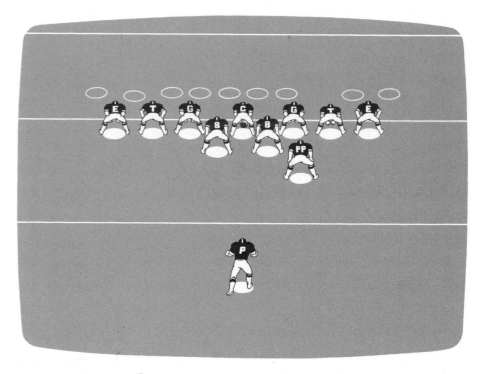

When the offensive team has not been able to gain ten yards in three downs, it almost always will give up the ball to the other team by kicking a punt (unless it is within field goal range). While the punt looks like a defensive play at first glance, it also has offensive implications. Since teams exchange offensive and defensive roles throughout the game by punting, the team with the best punting special team will gain net yardage on these exchanges.

The punting unit has two jobs: it must give the punter time to execute his punt, and then it must get downfield quickly and tackle the ball carrier as deep in his own territory as possible. While providing block protection for the punt is important, the more important job of the punting unit is to pursue the ball carrier and tackle him. For this reason, you will see a preponderance of defensive personnel in the punting formation.

■ THE PUNT FORMATION

The positions in the punt formation are the 'center' (C), the 'guards' (G) and 'tackles' (T), the 'ends' (E), the 'backs' (B), the 'personal protector' (PP), and the 'punter' (P).

The Center. It is far more difficult to center for the punt than it is to snap the ball into the hands of the quarterback, and for this reason the center for the punt is often a specialist who only comes in to center for the punt, field goal, and extra point. The center must be able to spiral the ball on the fly right into the hands of the punter. If the snap is not perfect—if it is high or low, or to the left or right—the punter may have difficulty catching the ball, causing him to have to rush his punt. Even worse, the punt could be blocked, the punter tackled before he gets the ball off, or the ball fumbled with the other team recovering.

The Guards and Tackles.
Attempts by the punt return team to block a punt come from the ends and through the middle, but the greatest rush usually is aimed straight through the middle, since that is the shortest distance to the punter. It is important, therefore, that the four linemen be strong, tough blockers who can hold up this kind of rush. Usually, the four line positions are filled by players who have the skills of linebackers or running backs because they are both strong enough to defend against the rush and fast enough to get downfield to cover the kick and get a crack at bringing down the punt return man.

The Ends. Only the two end men on the line are allowed to run downfield before the ball is punted; they may take off at the snap of the ball. Since the ends can get downfield quicker than anyone else, their main job is to tackle the punt return man. They must have great speed and the ability to tackle. Wide receivers, cornerbacks, free safeties, and, especially, strong safeties are desirable for these two positions.

Sometimes those ends will be closer to the sidelines than is shown in the illustration, much like the wide receivers in a standard offensive formation. You are likely to see this variation when the punting team wants to give the impression that it might be faking a punt. (Fake punts are rare, however.)

The Backs. The two backs are positioned behind the center so that they can stop the punt-blocking attack if an opponent gets past a lineman. Once the punt is off, the two backs must move downfield and tackle; therefore, they must be strong blockers to stop the punt rush, as well as good backup tacklers. You are likely to find linebacker types in these two positions.

The Personal Protector. The personal protector's first job is to protect the punter. If an opponent comes through the line and past the backs, or comes in from the side, the personal protector must stop him. After the punt is off, he must pursue the ball carrier. Usually you will see a linebacker playing this position.

■ THE PUNTER

Usually, the only job of the punter is to kick in punting situations. The punter stands about fifteen yards behind the line of scrimmage. Once he receives the snap from the center, he drops the ball and kicks it before it hits the ground. He does not punt with his toe, but with his instep — the area between his toe and the top of his shoelaces.

The punter strives for distance and hang time, just as the placekicker does. Hang time is important because the longer the ball is in the air, the more time the punting team has to get downfield in position to tackle the ball carrier.

Accuracy is also important. If the punt goes out of bounds, the return team must start play at the out-of-bounds point. For this reason, the punter often tries for a 'coffin corner' kick, aiming his punt out of bounds close to the return team's goal line and forcing it to start with a field position disadvantage.

The Punt Return

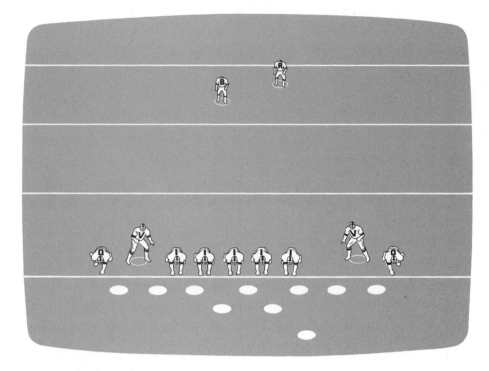

The punt return unit has one of two jobs. It can try to block the punt, or it can give a token rush while most of its players drop back at the snap to prepare for a punt return behind a wall or wedge. The decision as to whether the punt return team will rush to block or drop back to return is made prior to the play. We'll see how this is accomplished when we watch the kicking plays in the Third Quarter. Why a team will give maximum attention to the rush rather than the return will become apparent when we look at football strategy in the Fourth Quarter.

■ THE PUNT RETURN FORMATION

Since the punt return team does not want to tip off its strategy, it uses the same personnel regardless of whether the play call is for a rush or a setup for a return. There are various ways in which the punt return unit can align itself. A standard setup has nine men on the line or just behind it: five 'inside linemen' (I), two 'outside linemen' (O), and two 'rovers' (V). The backfield consists of a 'body-guard' (B) who blocks for the 'return man' (R).

The Inside Linemen. At the inside of the punt return unit are five players who will either rush forward to block or drop back to form a wall or wedge for the return. These inside men may assume a three-point stance, or they may stand upright like linebackers. These positions are played by offensive or defensive linemen or linebackers who have the speed and blocking ability needed to perform their designated jobs.

The Outside Linemen. The two men on the extreme ends of the punt return line are going to rush to block the punt from each side no matter whether the play calls for an all-out rush or a return. These players usually are men who are able to get in quickly from the outside and dive to block the punt. Wide receivers or cornerbacks generally play these positions because of their speed and agility.

The Rovers. Stationed just behind the punt return line are the two rovers. They will rush straight forward on a blocking play or drop back to cover the punting team's end men on a return play or a fake punt. Blocking ability and, especially, speed are needed for these duties, so free safeties or strong safeties line up in these positions.

The Bodyguard. The bodyguard is stationed in front of the punt return man. He will look upfield while the punt is in the air so he can see how fast the punting team is getting downfield, as it is part of his job to advise the punt return man whether to fair catch the punt or take it and run back. If it is a run-back situation, he must act as the return man's bodyguard and block for him. If it is a short punt, he must be able to fair catch it himself. Since ball handling and blocking are required for these chores, the bodyguard is usually a fullback type.

The Return Man. The first and most important job of the punt return man is to catch the punt. He must watch the ball into his hands, since a dropped punt is a fumble. After fielding the punt, he must have the blazing speed to make it upfield as far as possible. Punt return men belong to a specialist fraternity whose members are recruited for these qualities.

■ BLOCKING THE PUNT

The defense rushes and attempts to block the punt from the front and the sides. Once the defender has battled through the punting team's line, he aims his hands and body a yard in front of the punter. He does this for two reasons. First, this is the angle the ball will take as it leaves the punter's foot. More important, it is illegal for a defender to touch the punter unless the punt actually has been blocked or the punter breaks his natural rhythm either deliberately or accidentally — for example, on a fake punt or a bad snap from the center. If the defender misses the punt block and touches the punter, it is a roughing-the-kicker penalty, which allows the punting team to keep possession of the ball with a first down.

When a punt is blocked behind the line of scrimmage, it is a loose ball, and any member of either team who recovers it may advance it.

The Field Goal and Extra-Point Try

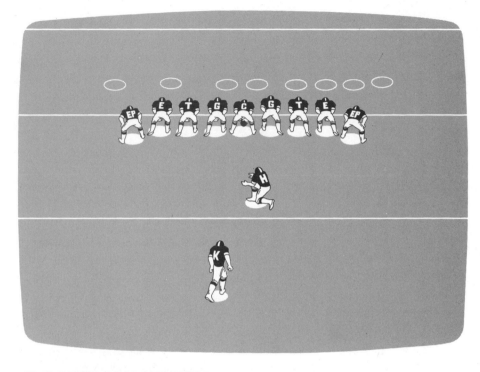

On any down, the offensive team can try to kick the ball through the goal post uprights for a field goal, scoring three points. After a touchdown, the scoring team may try for an extra point by either running or passing the ball over the goal line, or by kicking the ball through the uprights. In the pro game, the extra-point try is almost always a kick. For this reason, the field goal and extra-point try are similar offensive situations.

The field goal and extra-point unit is an important part of any football team. These players must combine their special skills to help get additional points on the scoreboard. Since many games are won by three or less points, this unit cannot afford to blow its scoring opportunities.

■ **THE FIELD GOAL AND EXTRA-POINT-TRY FORMATION**

The try for a field goal is made from the offensive team's line of scrimmage. The extra-point try is made by spotting the ball two yards from the goal line. Other than that, the formations for these two situations are basically the same.

The field goal and extra-point offensive formation puts the center (C) and two 'tackles' (T), 'guards' (G), and 'ends' (E) on the line, and two 'end protectors' (EP) about a yard back at either end of the line. A 'holder' (H) kneels on one knee about seven yards in the backfield and slightly to the right of the center. The 'placekicker' (K) stands back from where the ball will be placed on the ground by the holder so that he can approach the ball and boot it.

The Center. The center must have the same skills as those required for snapping the ball to the punter, but centering the ball for the extra point or field goal is even more difficult. The center must be able to spiral the ball back through his legs, right to the holder. If the snap is off, the holder can do little to adjust, since he is down on one knee. The player who centers for the punt also centers for the field goal and extra point; he is a specialist who is called upon to perform these critical chores.

The Linemen. Once the ball is snapped to the holder, it is the job of the center and the six linemen to hold back the defense until the placekicker has kicked the football. Their only job is to contain the rush to block the kick. These six positions are filled by strong, tall, and especially wide players.

The End Protectors. In order to protect the two sides, or ends, of the line, two players take positions in back of and at each end of the line. Their job is to stop any side rush-blocking attack by the defense. Good block protection ability is needed at these positions, so usually they are manned by offensive linemen.

The Holder. The holder must be able to catch the centered ball without bobbling it or fumbling it, so he must be a player who is used to handling the football. Usually he is either the team's first-string or backup quarterback. After he has taken the snap, he must place one point of the football on the ground, with the laces away from the kicker, and hold the ball in place until it is kicked. All this must be done as quickly as possible so the placekicker has the maximum amount of time to kick the football and the defense has the minimum amount of time to rush in to block the kick. This holding job is a specialized assignment requiring hours of practice each week.

■ THE PLACEKICKER (SOCCER-STYLE)

If each of the other players does his job correctly, the success of the field goal or extra point is up to the placekicker. Placekickers use either a toe kick, as we saw in the kickoff, or a 'soccer-style' kick. In the soccer kick, the kicker approaches the ball from the side and swings his leg around, meeting the ball with his instep. Players recruited from European soccer teams are now commonly used as placekickers.

The extra point calls for accuracy, and the field goal requires both accuracy and distance. Placekickers kick hundreds of extra points and field goals during practice each week. Their skills can make the difference between winning or losing every game the team plays. In fact, teams have won games by scoring only field goals and no touchdowns, and often a team's leading scorer is its placekicker.

The Field Goal and Extra-Point Defenses

There are different defenses for the field goal and extra-point try. The field goal defensive team tries to block the field goal attempt but it also must worry about a fake field goal, so some of its men hang back.

In pro ball, only one point is awarded for a point-after-touchdown try, and since the placekicker is a highly recruited specialist, it is considered relatively easy to make this conversion. So, in the pros, the extra-point defense is designed completely to block the kick.

In college and high school football, however, two points can be scored on the extra-point try by running or completing a pass over the goal line. Because of this, college and high school teams usually will use the standard field goal defense against the extra-point try as well, to protect against a fake kick.

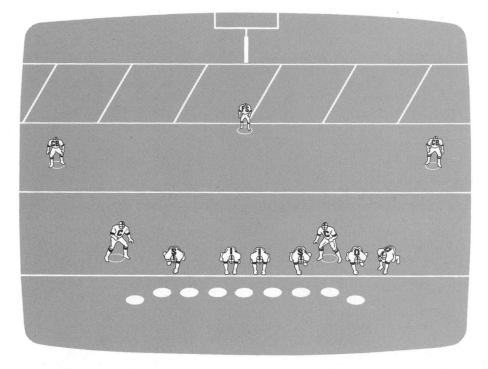

■ **THE FIELD GOAL DEFENSIVE FORMATION**

The field goal defensive formation is made up of two 'inside rushers' (I), two 'outside rushers' (O), two 'contain men' (C), two 'spies' (S), two 'cornerbacks' (CB), and one 'safety' (FS).

The Inside and Outside Rushers.
The two inside rushers must rush up the middle, much like defensive linemen do on a pass rush. Generally these positions are played by defensive tackles and nose guards.

The two outside rushers must be able to rush the field goal kicker in an attempt to block the kick, much as they would rush the quarterback on a passing play. The two outside rushers work as a team, with one man trying to attract a block so the other can attempt to get a piece of the ball. These two outside rushers are blitzing types such as linebackers and strong safeties.

The Spies and Contain Men.
Two men on the line of scrimmage act

as spies in case the field goal attempt is a fake that turns out to be a running or passing play. At the snap, they can move forward as if to block, but their primary job is to keep alert for a fake field goal. Since they must be able both to drop back and pass protect as well as to pursue a run, these players are usually linebackers.

The contain men, one on each side of the formation, must protect the sides of the field against a fake field goal. Linebackers usually play these positions as well.

The Cornerbacks and Safety. Behind the field goal defense's front line are the two cornerbacks and the safety. Since the man at each end of the field goal team's line, as well as the two end protectors, the holder, and the placekicker, are all eligible to catch passes, the three men in the defensive backfield must be alert to a fake field goal that turns out to be a passing play. Their primary assignment is to think "pass." Usually these positions are filled by the team's cornerbacks and free safety.

■ THE EXTRA-POINT DEFENSIVE FORMATION

The extra-point defensive formation is composed of three 'tall men' (T), four 'trail blazers' (B), two 'outside blockers' (O), a 'middle blocker' (M), and a 'jumper' (J).

The Tall Men. As the ball is kicked, all three of the tall men stretch out their hands and arms in an attempt to block the kick. The tall man on each side of the middle blocker also tries to open up a lane for the middle blocker so he has a shot at blocking the extra point. Usually these positions are filled by linebackers, but as the name implies, these players' main asset must be their height.

The Trail Blazers and Outside Blockers. The linemen next to the tall men act as 'trail blazers'. They try to block and move the extra-point team's ends and end protectors so that a path, or trail, is created for the two outside blockers. You will see linebackers in these positions.

The two outside blockers must get around the extra-point team's two

end men and end protectors and run in a straight line to a yard in front of the holder. There, they try to block the extra point by leaping in front of the holder with outstretched arms and hands. Since speed is needed at these positions, usually they are manned by cornerbacks.

The Middle Blocker and Jumper. The middle blocker is lined up in the gap between the extra-point team's center and guard. He tries to rush in through this gap to block the kick from

the middle. Since this move resembles rushing the passer, this man is likely to be a linebacker.

The jumper is stationed in the middle of the formation, opposite the spot where the ball will be held down on the ground for the extra-point try. He will jump up as high as he can to try and block the extra point. He must time his jump so that it coincides with the kick and its trajectory. A tall high-jumper is perfect for this position.

3RD QUARTER

Watching Plays

The halftime show is just ending, and we're ready to begin the Third Quarter. Now we're going to see how all the individual skills we watched in the first half of the game are put together into offensive and defensive plays.

By now we should realize that football is rarely a game of just individual effort; success is the result of many players, each doing a different job. On each snap of the ball, the offensive players, and to some degree the defensive players, have planned how they will work together to execute or foil a certain play in response to the game situation.

Our playbook contains basic running, passing, and kicking plays that you are likely to see in the game. They can be blocked or defended differently than we show them, but each of them is very much a standard play. We have frozen each of these plays at the point at which it is uncertain whether the offense or the defense will prevail.

Our description of the action assumes that you have watched the first half of this game with us. If you find the terminology or descriptions confusing, it's because you've skipped ahead and not read the First and Second Quarters — and that's a fifteen-yard penalty.

Inside Running Plays

As we'll see, inside running plays are aimed at the area of the line of scrimmage between the two offensive tackles. These are the fastest developing running plays and are used to plow ahead for short to medium yardage. They are also the 'safest' running plays for the offense, as there is virtually no open field running involved and the handoffs can be simple, or even avoided altogether.

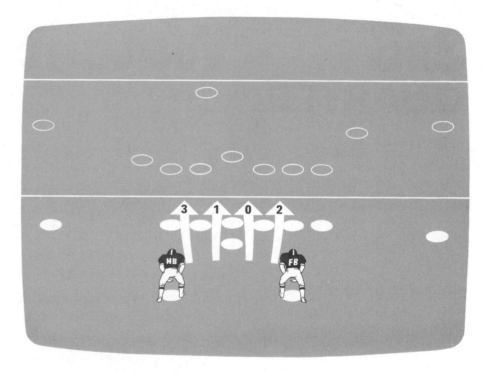

■ INSIDE RUNNING LANES

The running lanes or holes through which these plays are run are the number zero through three holes, between the tackles. The offense relies heavily on its interior line to make these plays work, and the defense depends on its down linemen to stop them.

There are three ways that these plays can be executed. A running back can take the handoff from the quarterback and run straight through one of the holes, a running back can take the handoff and follow the lead blocking of the other back through an assigned hole, or the quarterback can keep the ball and sneak through a hole opened in the line by his offensive linemen.

DIVE

The dive is a short yardage running play aimed through the line of scrimmage at the inside area between the two tackles. It is the simplest type of running play, as the halfback is not lead blocking interference and the offensive linemen execute straight ahead 'man' blocks.

Offense. At the snap, the right guard, right tackle, and tight end drive block straight ahead to push their opponents off the line. The fullback takes the handoff and plows forward through the biggest hole. The left side of the offensive line execute cutoff blocks to keep the defense to the weak side, while the center tries to block the middle linebacker so the fullback can break through.

Defense. The strong side defensive tackle, end, and linebacker must fight through the offensive blocks and plug up the holes quickly. If the middle linebacker can get past the block of the center, he can stop the offensive surge. Otherwise, it is up to the strong safety to halt the play.

BLAST

On this inside running play from the I Formation, the tailback takes the handoff and blasts through the area between the two offensive tackles behind the lead blocking of the fullback.

Offense. The right tackle and tight end must drive the strong side defensive end and linebacker off the line, but it is the blocks of the right guard and the fullback against the strong side defensive tackle and the middle linebacker that can really spring the play. The center and left guard co-op block the weak side defensive tackle; then the center must slide off this co-op block to block the pursuing weak side linebacker.

Defense. If the strong side defensive tackle and end can beat their blocks, the hole is plugged and the play is over. If not, the middle linebacker must come in and stack up the running lane. The next best bet for stopping the play is the strong safety. Note the weak side linebacker, cornerback, and free safety moving over to provide insurance.

■ QUARTERBACK SNEAK

The quarterback sneak is a short yardage play, expecting to get inches to a yard at best (although it is sometimes used as a trick play when longer yardage is needed). It is unique both because the quarterback keeps the ball and because of the wedge blocking.

Offense. First, notice that the offense is in a two tight end formation. At the snap, the line converges forward, forming a wedge for the quarterback, with the right guard the apex of the wedge. The quarterback plows ahead directly behind the right guard.

Defense. The defense expects this short yardage play, and is stacked with six men on the line, who drive under their offensive opponents to stack up the line. The middle linebacker must try to locate the apex of the wedge, break it, and jam up the hole. The secondary must guard against a trick pass play.

Off Tackle Running Plays

These plays can be run to the strong or weak side of the formation, either over or just outside the offensive tackles. Off tackle plays take longer to get underway than inside running plays since the ball carrier has a greater distance to travel to get to his running lane. Most of these plays involve lead blocking by a running back. They also frequently incorporate more complex blocking schemes by the offense.

■ OFF TACKLE RUNNING LANES

Off tackle plays can be run through the number four and five holes, or the holes directly over the offensive tackles if the team uses a 'man', rather than a 'gap', system for numbering its running lanes. The key offensive linemen on these plays are, as the name implies, the tackles, with help from the tight end and guards. Because the tight end is available to double-team block with the tackle, these plays are often run to the strong side.

The defensive ends frequently have important roles to play for the defense.

We'll look at three possible off tackle plays: one to the weak side, one to the strong side with a double-team block, and a 'power play' to the strong side with pulling guards.

■ OFF TACKLE (WEAK SIDE)

This is an off tackle play to the weak side utilizing co-op blocking. The full back will get the handoff and follow the lead blocking of the halfback through the running lane over the left tackle.

Offense. To open up the running lane, the halfback must block the weak side linebacker and the left tackle must hook block the weak side defensive end. In order to keep the middle linebacker from getting into position to make a tackle, the left guard must co-op block the weak side defensive tackle; then the left guard must slide off and cut off the pursuing middle linebacker. Notice that the split end is responsible for blocking the weak side cornerback.

Defense. The weak side linebacker must spot the direction of this play and beat his block. The weak side corner-back must keep the play to the inside, and the middle linebacker must get to the running lane quickly to provide fill. The last line of defense depends on the alertness of the free safety.

■ OFF TACKLE (STRONG SIDE)

On this off tackle play, the fullback lead blocks for the halfback, who runs through the lane to the outside of the right (strong side) tackle.

Offense. This is a simple off tackle play, where both guards block straight ahead rather than pull. At the snap, the right tackle and tight end double-team block the strong side defensive end, while the fullback leads to block the strong side linebacker. The halfback takes the handoff through the off tackle hole. Notice that the flanker tries to provide additional running room by slanting to take on the strong safety.

Defense. The strong side defensive end is trying to shut down one running hole by 'submarining' in response to the double-team block. The key to stopping the play is the strong side linebacker taking on the fullback, possibly with help from the strong safety. The cornerback must contain the play in case the halfback swings wide, and the free safety is the insurance man.

■ OFF TACKLE (POWER PLAY)

On this 'power play' through the strong side off tackle hole, the fullback carries the ball. He gets blocking help from a leading halfback, a double-team block, and a pulling guard.

Offense. Note the blocking scheme on this play. The right tackle and tight end double-team the strong side defensive end, as in the previous play, but the left guard pulls and comes around the strong side to block the middle linebacker. The strong side linebacker is blocked by the halfback. (If the strong side linebacker takes on the left guard, the halfback will have to take on the middle linebacker.) The flanker's assignment is to block the strong safety.

Defense. Again, the strong side defensive end is submarining against the double-team block. The strong side linebacker's reaction is the key to stopping the play behind the line. Stopping the play beyond that point depends on the reaction of the strong safety, strong side cornerback, and free safety.

Outside Running Plays

These running plays are aimed at the areas toward the sidelines, outside the offensive tackles. They take longer to develop, but allow the ball carrier to build up speed by the time he hits the line. Because these plays are aimed at a part of the field where there are fewer players at the snap of the ball, they can produce long yardage gains. They can also result in the offense being thrown for a loss if the ball carrier does not get a chance to 'turn the corner' and head downfield.

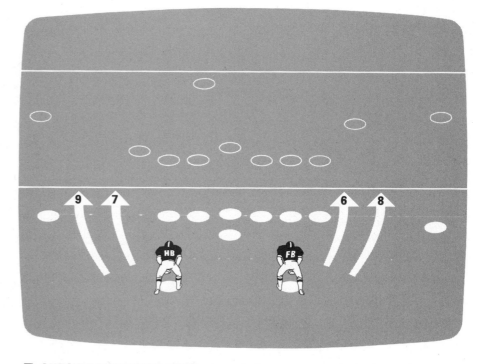

■ OUTSIDE RUNNING LANES

The outside running lanes are the number six through nine holes according to the system we've been using. Most of these plays will have the offensive guards pulling out of the line and moving over to provide blocking help for the ball carrier. On the defensive side, the outside linebackers frequently are called upon either to close the outside hole or to string the ball carrier out of bounds, with immediate backup help from the middle linebacker. The defensive secondary also becomes more of a factor in stopping these plays.

The three outside running plays we'll look at are a 'sweep' to the strong side, a strong side play utilizing a pitch-out, and a special outside play often seen in college games, the 'triple option'.

■ SWEEP

The sweep is run to the outside, between the tight end and the sideline. On this play, the halfback gets lead blocking help from the fullback and two pulling guards.

Offense. Notice how the offensive blockers work to clear the outside lane for the sweeping ball carrier. While the flanker slants to block the strong safety, the right guard pulls out and around to block the strong side linebacker and the left guard pulls to block the middle linebacker. The fullback is available to lead block against the strong side cornerback. On this play, the center, right tackle, and tight end block back toward the weak side.

Defense. As soon as the defense reads both guards pulling, they should think "sweep" in that direction. The middle linebacker and strong safety will try to string the ball carrier toward the sideline while the strong side cornerback forces containment.

■ PITCH

On this play, the tailback comes out of an I Formation, takes the pitch-out from the quarterback, and sweeps around the outside behind the leading fullback. The pitch allows the tailback to gain speed and momentum as he tries to turn the corner and get downfield.

Offense. The crucial offensive blocks are the hook blocks by the right tackle and tight end against the strong side defensive tackle and end, and the block by the pulling right guard against the strong side linebacker. The left guard pulls and cuts inside to block the middle linebacker. The flanker blocks the strong safety while the lead blocking fullback takes on the strong side cornerback.

Defense. The flow of this play is obviously to the strong side, and it will take some time to develop. If the strong side of the defense can read the play quickly, they can string it out and stop it. The weak side cornerback must cut across the field to provide insurance in case the tailback turns downfield.

■ TRIPLE OPTION

On the triple option, either the full-back, quarterback, or halfback carries the ball, depending on the reactions of the strong side defensive end, linebacker, and strong safety.

Offense. The quarterback takes the snap and moves to his right to meet the fullback, who is running over his right tackle. If the strong side defensive end does not converge on this hole, the quarterback hands off to the fullback. If, however, the defensive end does close this hole, the quarterback keeps the ball and moves to the hole over his tight end. If the strong side linebacker doesn't charge at the quarterback, he keeps the ball and runs through the hole. If the linebacker does charge, the quarterback pitches to the halfback, who runs a sweep.

Defense. The triple option works best if the strong side defensive end, linebacker, and strong safety are predictable. The offense can be stopped if these defensive players exchange assignments so the quarterback cannot read the defensive action.

Misdirection Running Plays

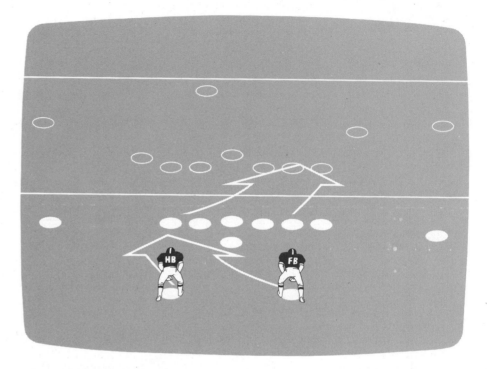

On misdirection plays, the offense tries to get the defense to commit itself in one direction while it runs the ball in the opposite direction. These plays are somewhat of a gamble. If the deception works, the play can result in a sizeable gain; if the defense is not fooled, the play is usually shut down. Misdirection plays work well on a wet or slippery field, as the defense often has trouble recovering from its initial reaction to the play flow.

■ MISDIRECTION PLAY FLOW

Although misdirection plays can be set up many ways, all involve blocking that flows in a direction opposite from the direction that the ball carrier takes. The ball carrier therefore ends up running away from the flow of the play. To make these plays work, the offense must give a strong showing with its blocking scheme to mislead the defense. This will usually involve blocking tricks by the offensive line, fake lead blocking by the running back, and often a false start by the ball carrier. If the defensive line and linebackers are fooled by the misdirection action, the defensive secondary is the last chance to stop the play.

Three misdirection plays we'll look at involve a ball carrier running counter to the play flow, cutting back against the offensive blocking, and a 'reverse' play with a double handoff.

COUNTER

This play utilizes two important concepts: misdirection running and trap blocking.

Offense. This play looks at first like a run to the weak side, with the center and left tackle blocking in that direction. The right guard steps back, giving the impression he is pulling. The fullback adds to the deception by pretending to lead block toward the left tackle. As the strong side defensive tackle is lured by the dropback steps of the right guard, the left guard pulls, cuts across the line, and trap blocks him. This opens a hole to the right of the center for the halfback to run through. Notice that the right tackle will block the middle linebacker away from the running hole.

Defense. If the strong side defensive tackle is not suckered by the trap block, the running hole will be closed. Even if the tackle is fooled, the middle linebacker can stop the play if he reads the misdirection action. Otherwise, the strong and free safeties must stop this run.

■ CUTBACK

This misdirection play demands a good fake lead by the fullback and running finesse by the tailback.

Offense. This play looks like a sweep to the right, with the entire offensive line and the fullback moving in that direction. Note that the right guard and tackle have reached toward the right, let their defensive opponents 'beat' them, and then wheeled these men to the right, out of the play. This is called 'reach and wheel' blocking. A key move by the left tackle is to let the weak side defensive end go by him and block the weak side linebacker. When the tailback gets the ball, he cuts back against the flow of the play and turns the corner on the weak side, past the committed defensive end.

Defense. The key to stopping the play is for the defense, particularly the weak side defensive end, to 'stay home' and not be fooled by the misdirection cutback. The middle linebacker can also stop this play if he avoids the block of the center. Otherwise, pursuit is up to the weak side cornerback and free safety.

■ REVERSE

This is a trick play. The quarterback hands off to the halfback, who runs right as in a sweep, then hands off to the flanker, running in the opposite direction. The flanker tries to carry the ball around the left side.

Offense. To make this play look like a sweep right, all the offensive blocking is initially pulled in that direction. After the flanker takes the handoff from the halfback, he must rely on the quarterback, left tackle, and left guard to block the weak side defensive end, linebacker, and cornerback. The split end blocks the free safety.

Defense. As this play takes a long time to develop, it can easily be stopped if the defense stays put and defends their assigned running holes. Since the weak side cornerback and free safety will likely have to stop this play, it is crucial how much they may have committed themselves to providing insurance toward the strong side.

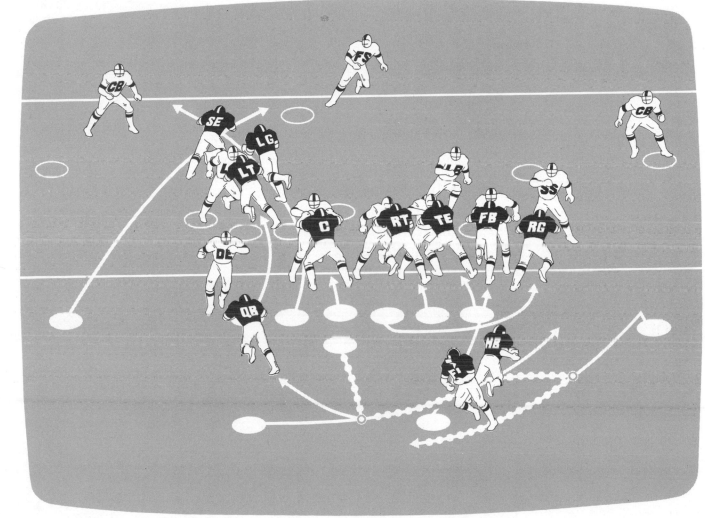

Run/Pass Action Plays

These plays all involve confusing the defense as to whether the play will be a run or a pass. Each of these plays starts out with action that looks like one type of play (run or pass), then turns into the opposite type. If a team has a 'balanced' attack — that is, poses both a strong running and passing threat — it can very effectively use these run/pass action plays to keep the defense off balance. The defense may tend to hold back committing itself to either a run or pass defense, and this can give an edge to the offense on every play.

■ QUARTERBACK FAKE

On all these run/pass action plays, the quarterback must give an Academy Award performance, with occasional supporting roles by his interior linemen. The key to fooling the defense as to the type of play is for the quarterback to execute a believable fake handoff when he is really going to pass, or to look like he is dropping back to pass when he really plans to hand off the ball or throw a short pass behind the line of scrimmage. The interior line must help by performing line blocking or pass drop protection as though it were the real thing. The defense must restrain itself from getting caught up in the act.

Three standard plays make up this run/pass action package: the 'play action pass', the 'draw' play, and the 'screen pass'.

■ PLAY ACTION PASS

The play action pass starts out looking like a running play and then turns into a medium- to long-range passing play. You'll see it often on first down and other running situations.

Offense. The two wide receivers and tight end run pass routes, but this does not automatically tip off the defense, as these players often run 'clearing' routes on running plays. At the snap, the interior line blocks to the right with the left guard pulling The quarterback fakes a handoff to his fullback, who pretends to follow the leading halfback. So far this looks like an off tackle or sweep running play. Then, the offensive line steps back to block for the quarterback, who scans downfield for his receivers.

Defense. The cornerbacks and safeties must be alert enough not to give up their pass coverage assignments by coming in to cover the pretended run. The play action pass aids normal running plays, as it tends to make the defensive secondary hesitant in playing pursuit.

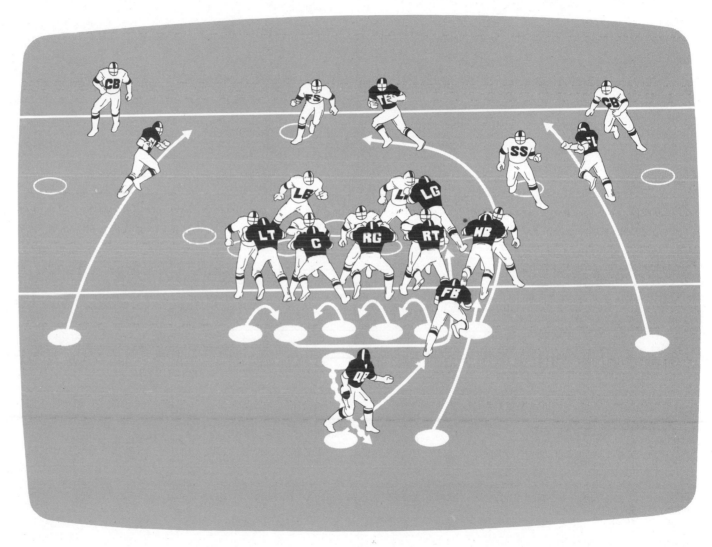

■ DRAW

The draw play fakes a pass and then turns into a run up the middle. Even if this play does not go for long yardage, it keeps the defense guessing on passing situations.

Offense. At the snap, the two wide receivers, halfback, and tight end run medium to long clearing pass routes to pull the cornerbacks, safeties, and weak side linebacker out of the play. The interior line also gives the impression of a passing play by dropping back to pass block and letting their opponents beat them. The quarterback drops back as if to pass and then hands off to the fullback, who runs up the middle past the defensive pass rushers.

Defense. The defensive pass rushers must sense that they are beating the offensive linemen too easily and read the draw. The key to the play is the middle linebacker. If he drops back to a zone pass defense as this fake passing play begins, the ball carrier can pick up good yardage.

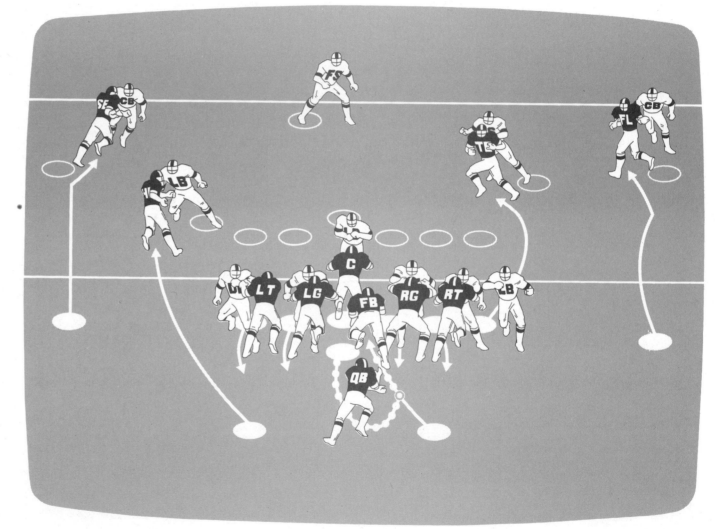

■ SCREEN PASS

The screen pass starts out like a passing play and then turns into a pass behind the line of scrimmage to the half-back. Since a running back receives the ball behind the line and picks up lead blocking, this is really a running play with the pass serving as a long handoff.

Offense. The split end, flanker, and tight end run long pass routes to clear the secondary. The quarterback drops back as if for a long pass while the interior linemen drop back with him. After giving token blocks to the rushing defensive linemen, the left tackle, guard, and center pull out of the pocket and swing left. The halfback stays back as if to block and then moves over behind them. The quarterback shoots a quick pass to the halfback, who moves downfield with his linemen giving blocking protection.

Defense. The weak side defensive end and tackle must stay with the offensive linemen as they make their sudden shift. Another key defender is the weak side linebacker, who will probably be playing zone pass defense. He has the best chance of stopping the play.

Short Passing Plays

We're going to look at some passing plays, following a slightly different format than we have for the running and run/pass action plays. First we'll look at a typical passing play consisting of five receiver routes, designed to gain either short, medium, or long yardage. Then we'll see how this play stacks up against some of the different pass defenses we looked at in the Second Quarter.

We'll first look at a short passing play that would be used to gain no more than about five yards. In the Fourth Quarter, when we watch football strategy, we'll see that certain situations arise in the game when it is fairly predictable that a short yardage passing play will be called. The defense will try to anticipate such a play and call an appropriate pass defense. The individual skills of the offensive and defensive players are certainly crucial, but the success of the play often turns on how the passing play and the pass defense match up.

■ SHORT PASS ROUTES

The short pass play we're going to look at consists of the following pass routes: The split end runs a square-out to the weak side; the halfback runs a shoot to the weak side; the tight end runs a slant-in to the middle; the fullback runs a shoot to the strong side; the flanker runs a square-out to the strong side.

The quarterback drop for this play is about three steps. This allows the receivers to get about five yards downfield before the quarterback fires his pass.

We'll now look at how this pattern works against three of the pass defenses we looked at in the Second Quarter. The activity we'll be looking at is precisely what the quarterback keys on as he 'reads' the pass defense.

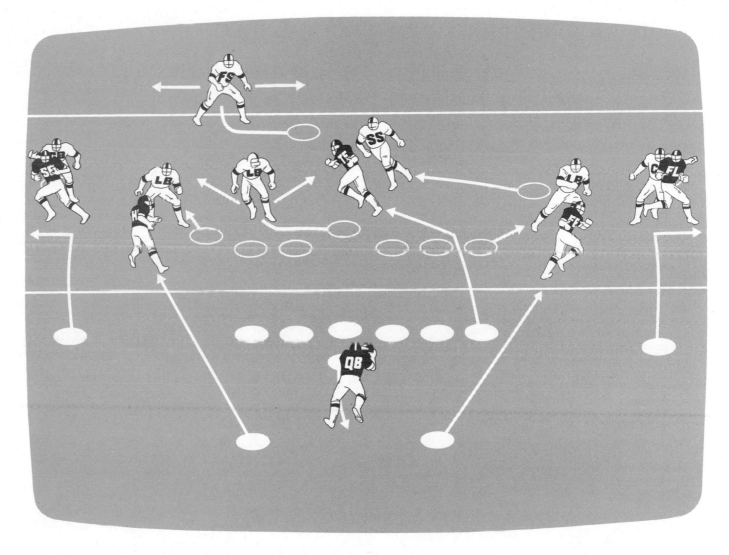

■ VS. MAN-FOR-MAN

This is the most basic man-for-man coverage. It is useful against short yardage situations, as all five receivers are covered and two men are free to help out.

Defense. The man-for-man assignments are as follows: The two cornerbacks cover the two wide receivers (split end and flanker); the two outside linebackers cover the two running backs (halfback and fullback); and the strong safety covers the tight end. The middle linebacker has overload responsibility; since the running backs are running routes to either side, he is free, as is the free safety. Here the middle linebacker is helping by covering the tight end to the weak side, while the free safety remains deep, but shades toward the weak side, in the direction the quarterback is looking.

Offense. The wide receivers and fullback are good targets if they can put a move on their defenders. The halfback and especially the tight end are running into heavy traffic.

■ VS. FIVE UNDER/ TWO DEEP ZONE

This zone coverage anticipates a short pass, as the short, or 'underneath', area of the defensive field is divided into five zones, rather than the 'normal' four.

Defense. Notice that the zone assignments follow a 'cornerback', or 'cloud', scheme, as the strong side cornerback is covering the strong flat zone, while the strong safety drops back to cover the strong deep zone. The free safety drops back to the weak deep zone. Since no routes are being run to the deep zones here, the free safety and strong safety will come in to provide backup coverage.

Offense. The offense is in fairly good shape here. The defensive call has given up two defenders to the two deep zones. All five receivers are threats to complete a short pass, although it may be difficult for them to continue for longer yardage.

■ VS. FIVE UNDER / THREE DEEP ZONE (3-4 DEFENSE)

This zone coverage makes full use of the extra linebacker that the 3-4 Defense provides. Since a quick pass is anticipated, the linebacker is more efficiently employed in the pass defense than rushing the quarterback.

Defense. The underneath zones are covered here by the four linebackers and the strong side cornerback. This leaves the weak side cornerback and the two safeties to parcel out the deep area into three zones. They will drop back to their zones at the beginning of the play and then move up to help where needed when they spot the five short routes.

Offense. The coverage of the five receivers is similar to the previous example, but note here that there is a backup defender for each potential receiver. Even if the pass is completed, there is no receiver who is likely to break away for longer yardage.

Medium Passing Plays

These passing plays are designed to pick up about ten to fifteen yards. They will be used when a specific amount of yardage is needed for a first down or as a surprise play action pass play when the defense is expecting a run.

The offense will try to anticipate the defensive pass coverage and employ pass routes that attempt to hit the 'seams' of the defense's zone coverage, or routes that send two receivers into one zone, 'flooding' the zone. The fact that the offense is often trying to 'dissect' the zone coverage heightens the offensive-defensive guessing game, and places a premium on the quarterback's ability to read the pass defense.

■ MEDIUM PASS ROUTES

The passing play we'll look at has three receivers running the primary routes: The split end runs a hitch come-back route to the weak inside; the tight end runs a deep hook route to the middle; the flanker runs a down-and-out route to the strong sideline.

The two running backs both run 'out' routes to the flat zones. These give the quarterback 'safety valve' targets in case the primary receivers are covered or his pass protection breaks down.

On passing plays, the wide receivers and tight end are often designated as 'primary' or 'secondary' receivers for the play. The quarterback chooses his receiver based on his reading of the defense. The quarterback will drop back about five yards before he selects his receiver and passes.

We'll now see how this play works against three of the pass defenses we looked at in the Second Quarter.

■ VS. DOUBLE COVERAGE

This pass defense is basic man-for-man coverage with double-team coverage of the split end.

Defense. The standard man-for-man coverage has the cornerbacks covering the wide receivers, the outside linebackers covering the running backs, and the strong safety covering the tight end. The middle linebacker is the 'overload' man and plays here as a free defender, available to help out in the underneath area. The free safety's assignment is to double-cover the split end with the weak side cornerback.

Offense. As with any man-for-man coverage, a lot depends on how well the receivers can put a 'move' on and get by their defenders, but the weak side of the field, with the double coverage and free linebacker, doesn't present very good targets. The best receiver is probably the flanker, with the fullback as a safety valve.

■ VS. FIVE UNDER MAN/ TWO DEEP ZONE

This pass defense is once again man-for-man coverage, with the addition of two defenders zoning deep.

Defense. The man-for-man coverage has the cornerbacks playing the wide receivers and the three linebackers playing the running backs and tight end. The two safeties drop back to cover the deep area of the field, in two zones, available to help the cornerbacks.

Offense. On this play, both wide receivers end up being double-covered by the pass defense. The quarterback will probably have to throw to one of his running backs or the tight end. Should either of these receivers spot the double coverage of the wide receivers they should come back toward the quarterback for the pass.

■ VS. STRONG SAFETY ZONE (3–4 DEFENSE)

This is a standard four under/ three deep zone defense, with one of the linebackers rushing the quarterback.

Defense. The strong safety plays the strong flat zone, so this is a 'strong safety', 'sky', or 'inverted' zone defense. The weak side cornerback, free safety, and strong side cornerback all move into the three deep zones in a 'strong rotation'. The strong side outside linebacker does not drop into pass defense, but rushes the quarterback. It is usual for one of the linebackers in the 3–4 defensive alignment to be committed to the pass rush.

Offense. The tight end has run his route to the seam of the two inside short zones and the middle deep zone. This effectively has drawn three defenders, leaving the wide receivers working against single coverage. The best passing opportunities are to the outside, with the halfback offering a good safety valve prospect.

Long Passing Plays

These seem to be the spectacular plays that everyone remembers, but they constitute less of the total game than the Monday morning paper would lead us to believe.

You'll see these 'bombs' thrown when a team is behind and needs long yardage quickly, or as a surprise tactic. In cases where long yardage is obviously needed, the defense is likely to be double-teaming the greatest receiver threats, or placing extra pressure on the quarterback with a blitzing pass rush.

■ LONG PASS ROUTES

The passing play we'll look at consists of deep routes by the primary receivers and medium and safety valve routes by the two running backs: The split end runs a square-out/corner route to the weak side; the tight end runs a curl-out/slant-in route to the inside; the flanker runs a deep post route to the strong side; the halfback runs a medium curl route and the fullback runs a down-and-out safety valve route to the strong side flat.

The quarterback will drop back about seven to nine yards before choosing his receiver and getting off the pass. This drop should give the primary receivers time to get downfield on their assigned routes.

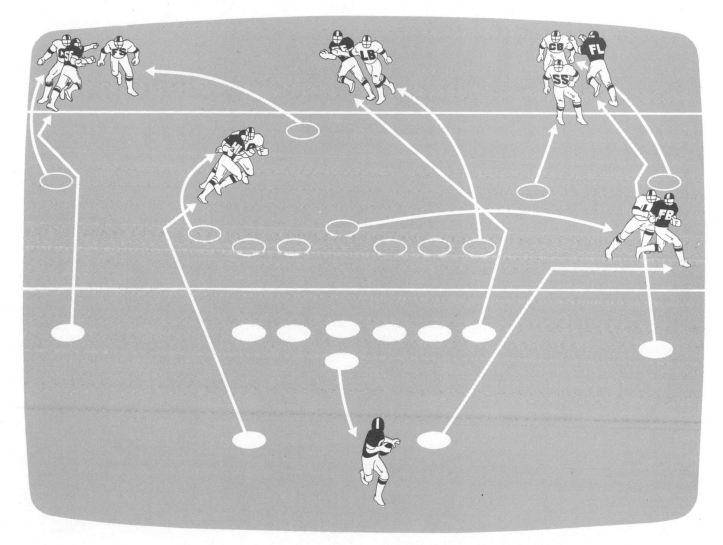

■ VS. DOUBLE-DOUBLE COVERAGE

This pass defense has both wide receivers double-covered on a man for man basis.

Defense. The weak side cornerback and free safety cover the split end, and the strong side cornerback and strong safety cover the flanker. The middle linebacker covers the tight end. The weak side linebacker covers the half-back, and the strong side linebacker's man assignment is the fullback.

Offense. The double-double coverage puts pressure on the wide receivers, but opens up the middle of the field. The tight end might be able to beat the middle linebacker. If all else fails, the safety valve route is likely to be open.

■ VS. FOUR DEEP ZONE

The defense is expecting the long pass and has assigned four zones in the deep area.

Defense. The deep zones are covered by the cornerbacks and the safeties. The three linebackers cover the underneath zones. Since this is zone coverage, both cornerbacks are trying to keep the wide receivers to the inside so they can have pass coverage help from the two safeties.

Offense. Here, the middle of the field is better defended. The tight end is closely covered, and the halfback will run into the middle linebacker even if he continues into the middle short zone. The wide receivers will have to contend mainly with their cornerback defenders.

■ VS. MAN-FOR-MAN—FREE SAFETY AND LINEBACKER BLITZ (3–4 DEFENSE)

Here the defense is responding to the threat of the long pass by putting extra pressure on the quarterback.

Defense. Normally one of the linebackers will rush the quarterback out of a 3–4 Defense. Here, the free safety as well as two linebackers are trying to surprise the offense by rushing with a blitz. This leaves the rest of the pass defenders to cover on a man-for-man basis. Notice that the cornerbacks try to keep the wide receivers to the outside on man-for-man coverage.

Offense. It's easy to see the gamble that the blitz entails. All of the potential pass receivers have only to beat their men, and there is no backup should they make a reception. On the other hand, the quarterback is in much greater danger. He may not have time for the receivers to complete their long pass routes, and may have to dump the ball or get sacked.

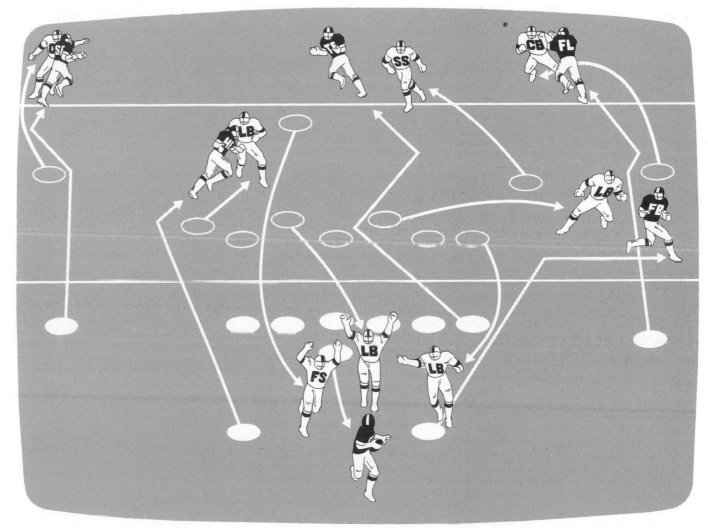

Kickoff Plays

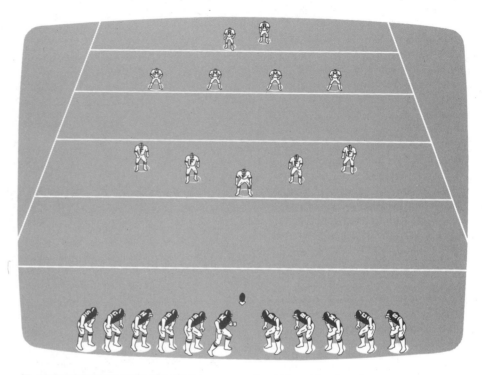

Since the kickoff return team can automatically advance to its own 20-yard line by downing the ball in the end zone, the measure of success for the return team is whether it can move the ball beyond that point. The goal of the kickoff team is to stop the return team behind its 20-yard line. The kickoff team players hope for a high, deep kick that will give them time to get downfield and set up a tackle.

When the kickoff team can't afford to give up possession of the ball, such as when it is behind at the end of the game, it will try an onside kick. We'll look at two variations of the onside kick play.

■ **THE KICKOFF AND KICKOFF RETURN FORMATIONS**

The kickoff and kickoff return formations we looked at in the Second Quarter are shown here lined up against each other. Notice that the kickoff team lines up with its eleven players — four wedge busters (B), two head hunters (H), two safeties (S), two contain men (C), and the placekicker (K) — spread across the entire field. The football rests on a kicking tee, spotted on the kickoff team's 35-yard line (40-yard line in college and high school). The placekicker starts several yards behind the ball.

The kickoff return team lines up in three waves: five front men (F) ten yards from the ball, four middle men (M), and two deep return men (R).

 **WEDGE RETURN**

This play illustrates the kickoff in a normal situation. The return team forms a blocking wedge up the middle for the return man. The kickoff team tries to bust through this wedge for a tackle.

Kickoff Team. Eight of the men on the kickoff team proceed down the field in two waves. The four wedge busters are expected to break the return wedge while the two head hunters try to get around the wedge to make the tackle. The two contain men keep the return man to the inside toward the wedge busters and the head hunters. The safeties and the placekicker hang back in case the ball carrier breaks loose.

Kickoff Return Team. The five front men block while the middle men back up and form a wedge for the return man who catches the ball. He must follow the wedge and not try to run away from it.

Another method of returning the kickoff is for the return team to form a wall up the side. We'll look at this maneuver when we look at punting plays.

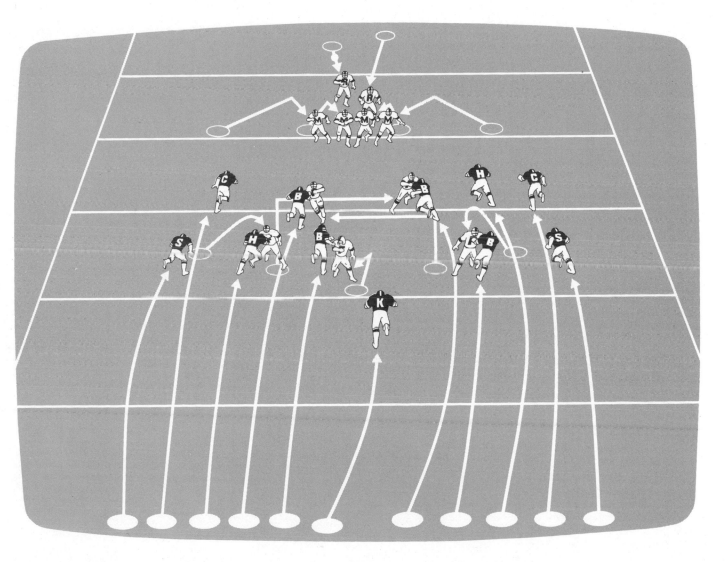

■ ONSIDE KICK

On the onside kick, the kickoff team tries to kick the ball at least ten yards downfield and then recover the football. You'll see this tried when the kicking team is so far behind that it must gamble on getting back the football.

Kickoff Team. The standard way to attempt this play is for the placekicker to kick the ball short to the middle of the field. The kicker tries to make the ball bounce along the ground so that it will be difficult to handle and to give his teammates at least a chance of recovering it. Both the kickoff and kickoff return teams will put players into the lineup who are used to handling the football, such as running backs, tight ends, and wide receivers.

Kickoff Return Team. All the return team must do is field the football and hold on, and it will have stymied the play while ending up in good field position. Once the ball has been touched by a member of the return team, even if it has not traveled ten yards, it may be recovered by the kickoff team.

■ ONSIDE KICK (SHIFT)

This variation on the onside kick play shifts some of the kickoff team's players to overload one side of the field.

Kickoff Team. Just before kicking the ball, the kicker yells, "Shift," and three of the players on the right side of the formation move to the left, positioning themselves next to the other five players on the left side of the lineup. Then the kicker kicks the ball to the left, in front of this group.

Kickoff Return Team. The shift is designed to surprise the return team and cause them to be outnumbered in the recovery attempt. It should be noted that if the ball is kicked in the air and one of the return team players has the presence of mind to signal for a fair catch while the ball is in the air, he must be allowed to catch the ball. Barring such sophisticated tactics, the onside kick play is likely to result in a mad scramble for the ball.

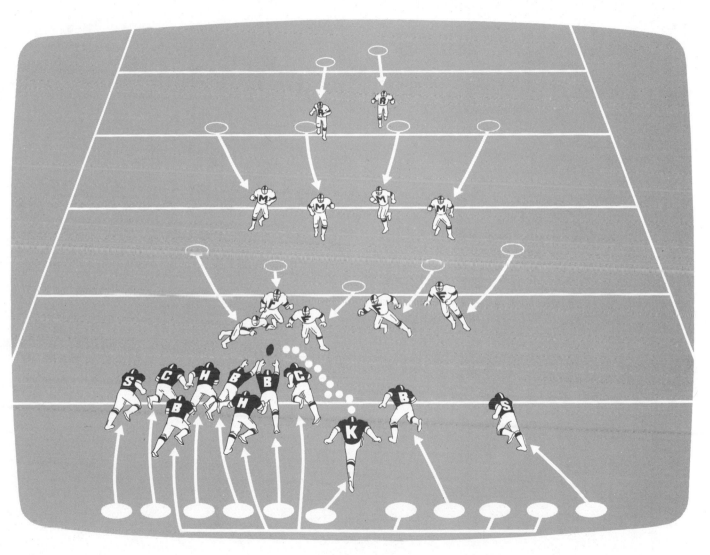

Punting Plays

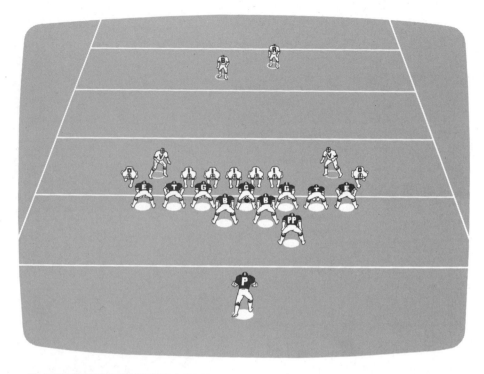

When a team faces a fourth-down situation and a field goal is out of its placekicker's range, usually it will punt rather than gambling on picking up the necessary yardage.

The punting team has two choices (other than faking a punt and going for the yardage). It can kick the ball high and deep, hoping for time to get downfield quickly and make a tackle, or the punter can attempt to kick the ball out of bounds between the opponent's goal line and 20-yard line so that the return team starts its offensive possession in poor field position.

The punt return team can either drop back and set up wedge or wall blocking for the return man, or it can put extra pressure on the line and try to block the punt.

■ **THE PUNT AND PUNT RETURN FORMATIONS**

The punt formation we looked at in the Second Quarter has a center (C) and two guards (G), tackles (T), and ends (E) on the line, and two backs (B) behind and to either side of the center. A personal protector (PP) stands behind the line to the right of the center, and the punter (P) about fifteen yards in back of the ball.

The punt return formation consists of five inside linemen (I), two outside linemen (O), two rovers (V), and a bodyguard (B) who blocks for the return man (R).

■ WALL RETURN

The punt has been kicked to the left side of the field, and the punt return team forms a wall up the sideline for the punt return man. The punting team tries to break through this wall for a tackle.

Punt Return Team. As the play starts, both the outside men rush in to put pressure on the punter. The two rovers drop back to opposite sides of the field to take on the punting team's two ends. The five inside linemen on the punt return team drop back to form a wall for the punt return man and his bodyguard.

Punting Team. The more quickly the punting team can spot the wall taking shape, the better chance it will have to break through it. Here, the left end and tackle try to get behind the wall to tackle the return man or run him out of bounds. The remaining players on the punting team try to break through the wall. The personal protector and punter stay back as the last line of defense.

The punt also can be returned with wedge blocking similar to that which we saw in the kickoff plays.

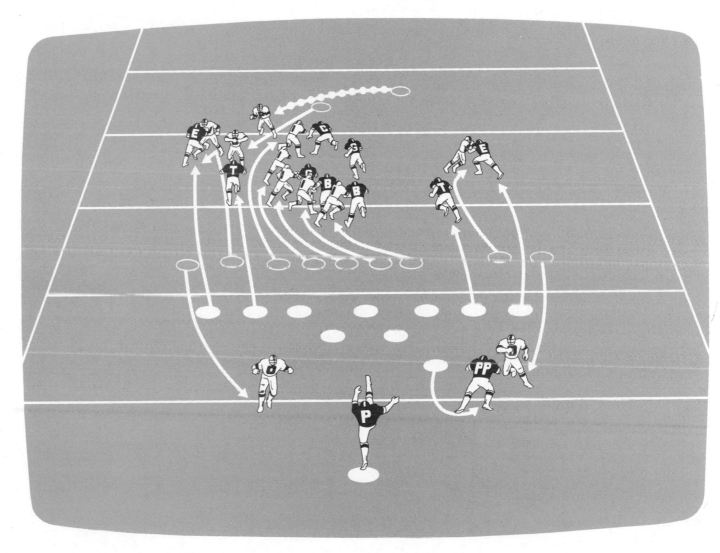

■ BLOCKING THE PUNT

Instead of dropping back, the punt return team can commit itself to blocking the punt by rushing from both sides and the middle. If the punt does get off, it is up to the punt return man and his bodyguard to do the best they can.

Punt Return Team. The return team sends eight men in to block the punt. Both outside linemen rush as usual, but they are aided by the inside linemen and one rover, who rush at the snap of the ball. The other rover doesn't rush; he stays free to help block for the return man in case the punt gets off. By and large, however, the return effort will have to be by the return man and the bodyguard without much help.

Punting Team. In this situation, the punting team has to worry less about getting downfield to cover the punt and more about holding off the punt block rush. If the punt is blocked, the only hope for the punting team is to recover the ball and advance it the distance necessary for the first down.

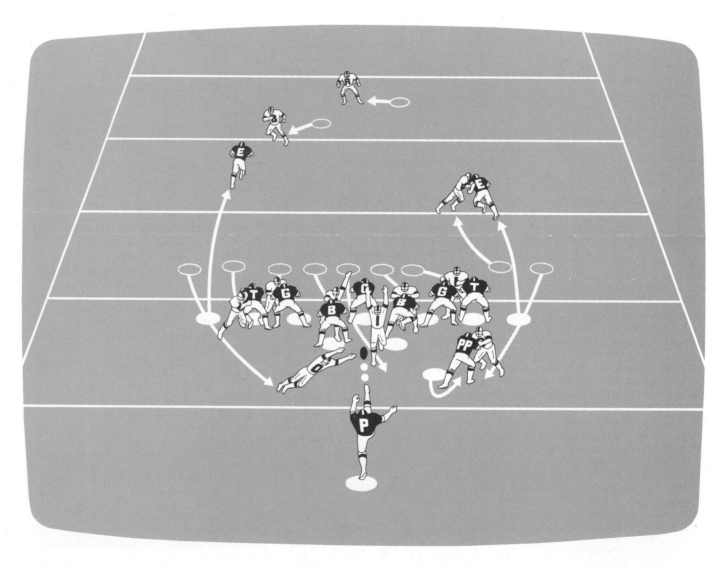

■ COFFIN CORNER KICK

If the punter is within range of being able to kick the ball out of bounds between the opponent's goal line and 20-yard line, he may try for this 'coffin corner' kick.

Punting Team. This is a tricky punt to try. If the punt goes out of bounds in the end zone, the return team gets the ball at its own 20-yard line. If the ball goes out of bounds at the sideline (say, the 30-yard line), the return team takes possession at the out-of-bounds spot. An inaccurate kick therefore might result in the return team starting its drive in much better position than if the ball were kicked to the center of the field. Sometimes a team will deliberately punt out of bounds to keep the ball away from a particularly dangerous return man.

Punt Return Team. If the ball goes out of bounds, the return team players have nothing to do but watch. They do, however, move toward the sideline where the punt is aimed so that if it is fielded by a teammate they can help block for him.

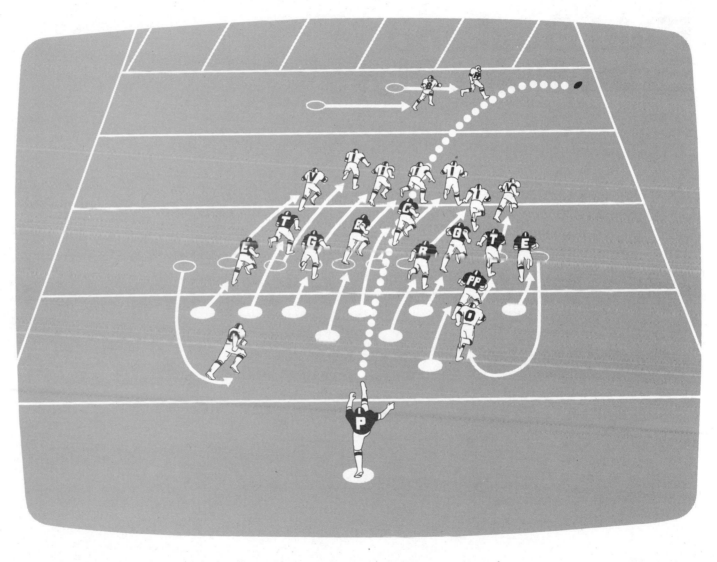

Field Goal and Extra-Point Plays

There are some situations where it is almost certain that the offense will try for a field goal. At other times, however, depending on the team's field position, the score, and the time remaining in the game, there is a possibility that the offense will fake a field goal and run or pass the ball. The field goal defense has to stay alert to this possibility.

In professional football, where only one point may be gained on the extra-point try regardless of whether the ball is kicked through the uprights or run or passed across the goal line, and where kickers are very accurate, the extra-point play always involves an attempt to block the kick. In college and high school ball, the defense must be alert to the possibility of a two-point conversion via a run or pass.

■ THE FIELD GOAL OFFENSIVE AND DEFENSIVE FORMATIONS

Regardless of whether the offense is trying for a field goal or an extra point, it will line up in the same formation, with seven linemen (C, G, T, E), two end protectors (EP), a holder (H), and the placekicker (K).

The field goal defense, illustrated here, has eight men on the line, consisting of two inside linemen (I), two outside linemen (O), two contain men (C), and two spies (S). There are three men in the backfield: two cornerbacks (CB) and a safety (FS). This defensive alignment also is used against the extra-point try in college and high school ball.

■ FIELD GOAL—OUTSIDE RUSH

The field goal defensive team is rushing from the side as well as the middle to try to block the kick, while still playing safe in case of a fake.

Field Goal Defense. The key men in this play are the two outside linemen. The extreme outside lineman tries to get a yard in front of the holder so he can leap with arms and hands outstretched to block the kick. He is aided by the outside lineman next to him, who tries to attract the block of the end protector. The two inside linemen rush in through the gaps on each side of the center with their hands up in an attempt to get a piece of the ball. The rest of the defensive unit is alert to the threat of a fake, with the two contain men guarding the close sides, and the two spies ready to drop back to help the cornerbacks and safety guarding the deep outsides and middle.

Field Goal Offense. The entire effort of the field goal offensive team is to keep the rushers at bay and give the kicker as much protection as possible to execute an accurate kick.

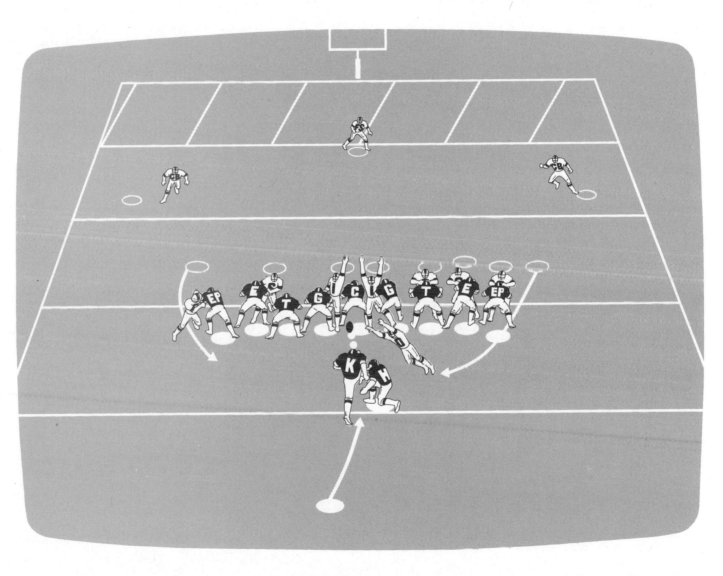

■ EXTRA-POINT BLOCK

The extra-point try in the pros has all defensive players acting in concert to try and block the kick. The defensive alignment (described on page 145) dispenses with the backfield positions in favor of more linemen.

Extra-Point Defense. The two outside linemen (O) attempt to get in and block the kick with the help of the four trail blazers (B), who try to attract the blocks of the offensive team's ends and end protectors. The middle man (M) also attacks, with two of the three tall men (T) trying to help open a path for him. The other tall man and the jumper (J) leap as high as possible with their arms up to try and deflect the football.

Extra-Point Offense. The extra-point conversion is expected to proceed like clockwork. The center must get off an accurate snap right to the holder, who must set the ball down quickly, hold it steady, and let the kicker send the ball high over the defense and through the uprights. The line and end protectors must thwart the rush of the defense.

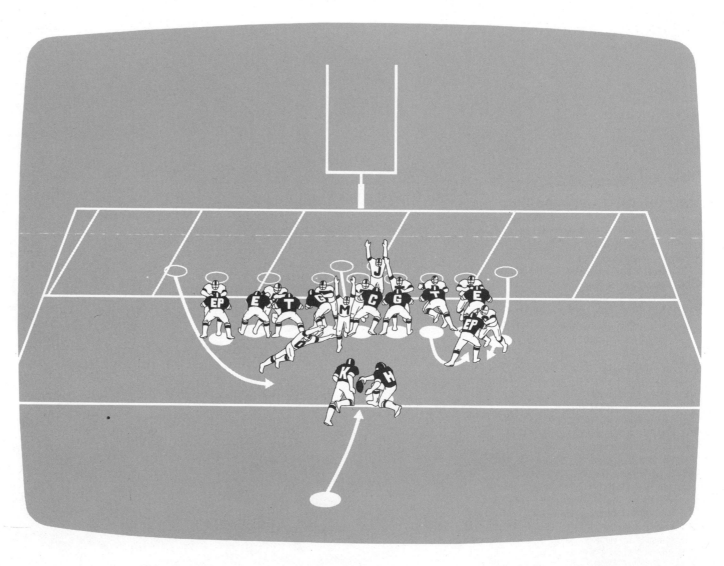

■ TWO-POINT CONVERSION

This is a play to gain two extra points following a touchdown in college or high school football, by passing or running the ball over the goal line. It is run out of a standard extra-point kick offense.

Extra-Point Defense. Since the try for a two point conversion is a possibility, the defense aligns itself as it would to defend against a field goal. The outside and inside linemen rush, while the contain men protect the sides and the spies stay alert for a run or pass through the middle. The cornerbacks and safety stay back.

Extra-Point Offense. The center snaps the ball, not to the holder, but directly to the placekicker. As the place-kicker rolls out to the left, the left guard pulls to provide blocking protection along with the holder. The left end and end protector slant to flood the left corner of the end zone. The ball-carrying place-kicker has two blockers and two receivers in front of him. He can either run or pass, depending on whichever develops as the better option.

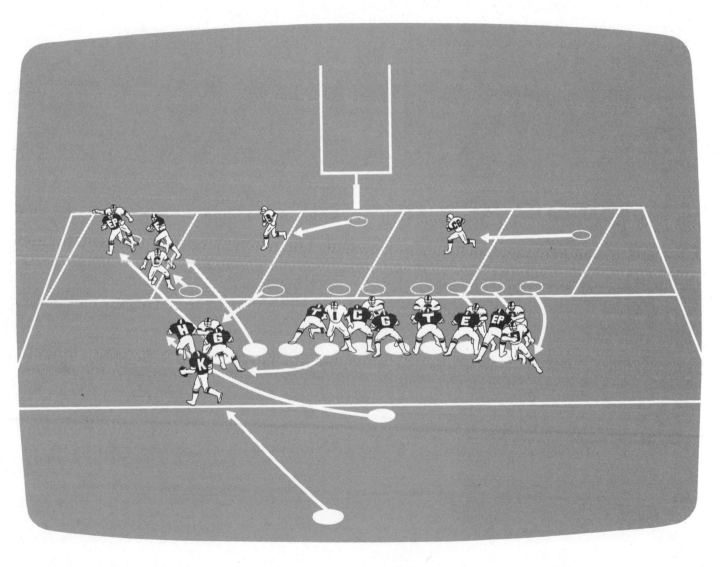

4TH QUARTER

Watching Strategy

This has been almost as busy a game for us as it has been for the players. In the First and Second Quarters, we watched the offensive, defensive, and kicking teams. In the Third Quarter, with the help of our playbook, we watched the offense and defense interact with basic plays. During this quarter, we're going to sit back and take the coaches' view as we watch the two teams put their strategies into operation.

First, we'll look at the notion of playing 'percentage football'—understanding the overall chance of success with different types of plays. We'll see how this notion is applied in different field position, down number and yardage, and time and score situations. Then we'll look at how individual and team tendencies affect these abstract principles, and how teams scout for these tendencies. Finally, we'll see how coaches put together a game strategy by looking at some of the competing philosophies of football.

To some extent, we might be able to 'predict' what the next play might be, based on all these considerations. Our real purpose during this quarter, however, is to understand when a team is playing by the percentages and when it is choosing or being forced to gamble.

Percentage Football

There are three principles that form the foundation of playing 'percentage' football. The first is that the offensive team must gain at least ten yards in three downs. The second is that it is safer to run with the football than it is to pass it. The third principle is that a completed pass will, on the average, yield more yards than a run. A team may not always play according to the implications of these principles because of the game situation or the team's evaluation of its own or its opponent's strengths and weaknesses; nevertheless, these three basic considerations are at the root of all strategic decisions.

■ TEN YARDS NEEDED IN THREE DOWNS

The rules of football require a team to gain ten yards in four 'downs', or plays, in order to be awarded a 'first down' and the opportunity to retain possession of the football for another four downs. As a practical matter, however, a team really must pick up these ten yards in *three* downs, rather than four.

It is considered too big a gamble for a team to continue to try for yardage if it has fallen short of gaining ten yards in three downs. If a team tries and fails to gain the needed first-down yardage on fourth down, it must give up the football to its opponent at the spot where it failed to make this fourth-down pickup. Consequently, a team usually will punt away the football on fourth down. The average punt in professional football is about thirty-seven yards and the average punt return is about nine yards. Therefore, the offense would, in effect, give up twenty-eight yards to the defense if it tried for a first down on fourth down and failed.

When a team thinks it is close enough to score a field goal, it will try for the field goal on fourth down rather than punting, but even that is a gamble. If the field goal fails, the opposing team takes over possession of the ball at the line of scrimmage from which the field goal was attempted (or at the 20-yard line if the attempt was from inside the twenty).

In any case, a team has to pick up about 3.3 yards per play if it is going to keep its scoring drive moving. How the team goes about doing this is affected by the other two principles of percentage football.

Percentage Football

AVERAGE PUNT	37 YARDS
AVERAGE PUNT RETURN	9 YARDS
AVERAGE RUN GAIN	3 YARDS
AVERAGE (COMPLETED) PASS GAIN	7 YARDS
PASS ATTEMPTS INCOMPLETE	49%
SEASON RUNNING TURNOVERS	43%
SEASON PASSING TURNOVERS	57%

■ SAFER TO RUN THAN TO PASS

The second principle is that it is safer to run with the football than it is to pass it. There are two reasons for this. First, a team can expect to gain at least some yardage by running the ball, while an incomplete pass nets zero yardage. On the average, a running play gains about three yards, while forty-nine percent of passes are incomplete. If a team runs the football, it can expect three yards; if it passes, there is about a fifty-percent chance that it will end up with nothing. Since a team needs ten yards in three downs, an incomplete pass puts a team in the hole in its attempt to pick up first-down yardage.

The second reason it is safer to run than to pass is because more turnovers occur when passing the football than when running with it. Of all the turnovers that occur in a season, about fifty-seven percent are interceptions and forty-three percent are lost fumbles. Consequently, there is less chance of losing the football by a turnover if a team keeps the ball on the ground.

■ MORE YARDS GAINED PASSING THAN RUNNING

Even though we have seen that it is safer to run with the football than to pass it, the average passing play that does result in a completion gains more yardage than the average running play. While a running play averages a gain of about three yards, a completed passing play averages a gain of about seven yards. Since a team needs to gain an average 3.3 yards per play, if it is behind in gaining first-down yardage, it must resort to the higher yield (but higher risk) passing play to make up the difference.

■ STATISTICS

Much of the strategy of football is based on statistics, but before going further we should caution you that statistics can often be misleading. For example, if a team ran a particular play one hundred times during a season and gained five hundred total yards, it would have averaged five yards per play with that play. On the surface, that looks very good. But if, in fact, all five hundred of those yards were gained on just ten of the hundred plays and no yards the other ninety plays, all we could say is that this was a spectacular, but not very consistent play. The really meaningful statistic is how successful a play is likely to be each time. If, for example, a play gains at least four yards eighty percent of the time, it is obviously a very efficient play.

Field Position

How often have you heard a commentator say that a team has good or bad 'field position'? Field position is the spot on the field where the offensive team will begin its next play and is considered 'good' or 'bad' depending on how far the team is from its opponent's goal line and a scoring opportunity. The further away the offensive team is from its opponent's goal line, the poorer the offensive team's field position; as the offense gets closer to the defensive team's goal line, its field position becomes better.

It is important to understand the strategic implications of field position because the offensive team chooses its plays based on whether it has good or bad field position, and the defense adjusts its defensive coverage according to the field position of its opponent.

■ PSYCHOLOGY

Before we examine the details of field position strategy, we should at least mention the psychology of field position. The offense can expect the defense to play loose when the offense is between its own goal line and its 40-yard line, because of the distance it has to go for a touchdown. When the offense is between the two 40-yard lines, the defense is likely to be more apprehensive and to tighten up. And, when the offense is between the defense's 40-yard line and the goal line, the defense is thinking, "Hey, we could get burned here," so the defense will probably play its tightest football in this area. Consequently, the offense can expect better defensive concentration as it gets closer to a score. Of course, the defense tries to fight against these psychological tendencies, but since they are psychological, they are difficult to avoid.

■ TURNOVERS AND SCORING OPPORTUNITIES

Field position strategy is primarily concerned with fumbling or interception turnovers, and with scoring opportunities. The closer a team is to its own goal line, the more conservative its decisions will be in terms of turnover potential. As a team approaches the middle of the field it is more apt to gamble, but it will become conservative again as it approaches its opponent's goal line, as it will want to protect its field goal or touchdown scoring opportunity.

The principle underlying field position is: "Don't let your opponent start its offensive drive in better field position than you are in when you give up the football." In other words, if a team is forced to punt, or risk a turnover, it wants that outcome to place the opposition in poorer field position (from the opposition's standpoint) than its own field position was when the play began.

Field Positions

■ THE SIX FIELD POSITIONS

To understand how field position affects the strategic play of the offense and defense, we will look at six offensive field positions.

• 'Very poor' field position: between the offense's goal line and its 5-yard line

• 'Poor' field position: between the offense's 5-yard line and its 20-yard line

• 'Mediocre' field position: between the offense's 20- and 40-yard lines

• 'Average' field position: between the two 40-yard lines

• 'Good' field position: between the defense's 40- and 20-yard lines

• 'Excellent' field position: between the defense's 20-yard line and its goal line

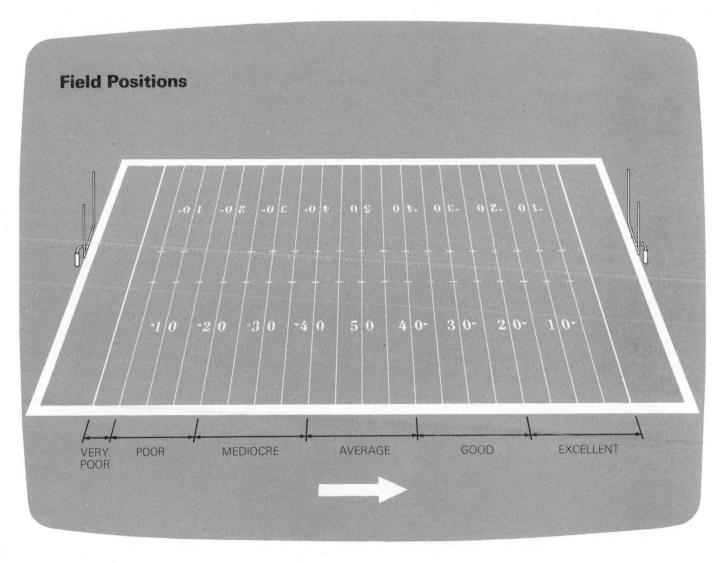

VERY POOR   POOR   MEDIOCRE   AVERAGE   GOOD   EXCELLENT

■ VERY POOR FIELD POSITION (GOAL TO 5-YARD LINE)

If the offense fumbles and turns over the football in this field position, it probably will have to concede a field goal, if not a touchdown, to its opponent. Thus, safety is the prime consideration for the offense in this portion of the field.

You will not often see the quarterback pitch out or fake a handoff in this area; instead he will want to safely hand off the ball to his best running back and let him dive or blast up the middle, or run off tackle behind his best blockers. Sweep plays also are too risky in this position; they take too long to develop. A quarterback sneak is a safe play that you might see in this situation. You also can expect to see a two-tight-end formation, since this aids the execution of inside and off tackle runs. The possibility of being caught behind the line of scrimmage must be reduced to nothing in this terrible field position.

In very poor position, the offense must try to get some working room, but passing is a big gamble. The quarterback has to drop into his end zone to pass, and a sack there would give the defense a 2-point safety. An offensive holding penalty in the end zone also results in a 2-point safety. If a short or medium pass is thrown and the ball is intercepted, the opponent is in position for an easy field goal or potential touchdown. If the offense does gamble and passes, you will likely see a long play action pass, where a potential interception would not be as disastrous.

It is important for the offense to gain some yardage in this situation because it might have to punt. The punter is used to punting from fifteen yards behind the line of scrimmage. The end zone is ten yards deep, and it is illegal for the punter to punt from outside the end zone. So, in this field position, the punter would have to stand closer than his normal fifteen yards, which would throw off the timing of the center snap and give the punter less room for protection. If the ball is punted from very poor field position, the opposition is likely to start its offensive drive in good field position.

■ POOR FIELD POSITION (5- TO 20-YARD LINES)

Field position between the offense's own 5- and 20-yard lines is not much better than very poor field position, but at least there is a little more room to maneuver. Now you may see the quarterback fake a handoff to fool the defense, but he probably will avoid pitching out because of the risk of a fumble. Essentially, you'll see the offense employ simple handoffs and try to run the ball up the middle or perhaps try an off tackle play.

Passing is still risky. If the quarterback does throw the ball, it is likely to be with 'quick out' short passes and slant routes. The offense also might gamble on a long play action bomb, which, if intercepted, would at least force the opposition to start its offensive drive deep in its own territory, in poor or mediocre field position. In that sense, an intercepted long pass would be comparable to the offense punting.

■ MEDIOCRE FIELD POSITION (20- TO 40-YARD LINES)

From mediocre field position, you will see the offense open up its running game, but it still will have to be conservative about passing. The offense is still four to five first downs away from a field goal try, and, if forced to punt, the defense could take over in average field position.

You can expect to see the offense use all its running plays, and the screen pass, which is essentially a running play to the outside with the screen pass serving as a long handoff. Short passes, especially in the middle of the field, are dangerous, since an interception would put the opposition in good field position. If the offense passes, you will likely see the quarterback throw short flat passes and medium-range sideline passes, or the high yield (but low percentage) long bomb.

■ AVERAGE FIELD POSITION (40- TO 40-YARD LINES)

This area of the field is considered average field position because most of the game is played between these two yard lines. If you are watching a game that is being played on a grass field, look at the turf in this area and you will see that there is more dirt there than grass, because this area of the field gets the most use.

When you see a team in average field position, you can expect it to open up and play its entire game. Even an interception from this field position isn't the disaster it is from worse field positions. If there is an interception, the offense's opponent would have to start in the hole as far as field position is concerned. So, you can look for the full repertoire of the running and passing games.

If forced into a fourth-down punting situation, the punter has a shot at a coffin corner kick from this field position. If successful, this would force the opposing team to start its offensive series in very poor field position.

This is the first field position situation that we have looked at that puts real pressure on the defensive squad. They must play tight and expect anything, while in previous field position situations they could expect the offense to be relatively conservative.

In this area of the field, the down number and yardage needed for a first down are likely to be major factors in the type of play the offense calls. We'll look at these considerations in the next section once we've looked at the good and excellent field positions.

■ GOOD FIELD POSITION (40- TO 20-YARD LINES)

When you see the offense with the football between its opponent's 40- and 20-yard lines, you are seeing a team in good field position. From this area of the field the offense is in reasonable field goal range and within striking distance of scoring a touchdown. Even if it loses possession of the football at this point, the opposition will have to take over in poor or mediocre field position. Don't, however, expect the offense to go hog wild and gamble. Since it is close to a sure 3-point field goal, the offense will want to make sure it doesn't turn over the football with a fumble or interception. You can expect to see both running and passing plays from this field position, but nothing too crazy.

■ EXCELLENT FIELD POSITION (20-YARD LINE TO GOAL)

When the offense is in excellent field position, it is the defense that has its back to the wall. The offense has almost a sure field goal and is close to scoring a touchdown. You are likely to see the offense run the football from this spot, because it doesn't want to risk losing its field goal opportunity by an intercepted pass and because there is not much area of the field left for passing. (A pass has to be caught in the end zone, and not out of it, if it is to be ruled complete and a touchdown.) In this area of the field, the offense is likely to 'break' formation, using double wings, triple wide receivers, and shifts and motion, all in an attempt to get the defense to play the offense's game.

The defense is likely to assign one 'hit man' just to cover the quarterback. This puts extra pressure on the quarterback in passing situations and guards against a bootleg run. It is difficult for the defense to execute zone pass coverage with so little area of the field left.

Down Number and Yards to Go

You have probably heard a commentator refer to a play as a 'third and long' or 'second and short' situation. These terms are another key to percentage football. What the offense is likely to do and what the defense expects is based on the offense's field position, the down number, and the number of yards the offense must pick up to make a first down.

We'll look at eight down number and yards-to-go situations that a team faces. Its decision as to what type of play it will call varies according to these situations. Later, when we look at team tendencies, we'll see how teams choose different types of plays — for example, a strong side sweep over a weak side sweep in a particular situation. For now, let's see how the down and yardage situation influences a team to run, pass, punt, or try a field goal.

■ FIRST AND MORE THAN TEN

The first down and more than ten yards to go situation occurs when the offense receives a penalty on a first-down play and the defense accepts that penalty. With more than ten yards to go, the offense is obviously in a hole in trying to pick up a first down. In this situation you almost always will see a pass, as extra yardage is needed. With the defense expecting a pass, the draw and screen plays are also possibilities.

The exception might be if the team is in very poor or poor field position. In these situations, the offense is afraid of an interception so close to its own goal line and usually will run the football and hope for the best. The offense is also likely to be wary about passing on the first down and more than ten yards to go situation when it is in excellent field position, as it will want to protect its field goal opportunity.

■ FIRST AND TEN

The first and ten situation is usually a running play. If the team can run for more than three yards, it will be in a position to be able to try another running play. If the team passes and the pass is incomplete, it really will be forced to pass again, as it will be minus the average of about three yards that usually is picked up on a running play. Remember that a running play is a higher percentage play than a passing play; in most cases, at least some yardage is gained on a run, but a pass that is incomplete gains nothing.

You also will see play action passes on first and ten situations, because the defense is expecting a run. Such a play might fool the defense, but it is still more of a gamble than a running play. Curiously, statistics show that, while the most frequent down number and yards-to-go situation is first and ten, the second most frequent situation is second down and ten yards to go. These statistics show how frequently teams play action pass on first and ten, and how frequently these play action passes are incomplete.

Down and Yardage Situations

FIRST AND MORE THAN TEN	PASS
FIRST AND TEN	RUN / PLAY ACTION PASS
SECOND AND LONG	PASS
SECOND AND MEDIUM	RUN
SECOND AND SHORT	PASS
THIRD AND LONG	PASS
THIRD AND SHORT	RUN
FOURTH DOWN (AVERAGE OR WORSE POSITION)	PUNT
FOURTH DOWN (GOOD OR BETTER POSITION)	FIELD GOAL TRY

■ SECOND AND LONG (7+ YARDS)

Second down and seven or more yards to go is considered 'second and long'. In this situation, the offense gained less than 3.3 yards on the first down. Now it is behind its needed average gain; it must gain at least four yards on this down.

Because it is behind on the needed per-play yardage, you often will see the offense try a short or medium pass in this situation. The exception to this is when the team is in very poor, poor, or in excellent field position. If in very poor or poor field position, the team might be reluctant to pass and risk an interception so close to its own end zone. If a team is in excellent field position, it might not want to pass and risk an interception when it is so close to an almost sure 3-point field goal.

■ SECOND AND MEDIUM (3 TO 6 YARDS)

This is a situation not usually mentioned by TV commentators, but it is useful in understanding football strategy. If a team possesses the ball on second down and three to six yards to go, it has exceeded its needed average gain on the first down. Therefore you can expect the offense to continue to run with the football, although it might try and surprise the defense with a play action pass. If in excellent field position, the offense probably will keep the ball on the ground to protect the field goal opportunity; in very poor or poor position, it will do the same because an interception in this area could result in a field goal or touchdown for the opponents.

■ SECOND AND SHORT (−2 YARDS)

Second down and short yardage of two or less yards to go for a first down is almost a sure bet for the offense to gamble on a passing play since it is ahead of its needed average gain. This situation is frequently called a 'throw-away' down. The only exception is when the team is in excellent field position and near the goal line and wants to protect a sure field goal by not putting the ball in the air and risking an interception.

■ THIRD AND LONG (3 + YARDS)

In the third and long situation, the offense needs three yards or more to gain a first down. It almost always results in a passing play. This is a do-or-die situation for the team to make a first down, or it will have to punt the ball away.

If in poor field position, a team may elect to run on third and three or four yards to go, in hopes of getting lucky and picking up the first down without passing and risking an interception. Also, a team in excellent field position may elect to run and protect the field goal rather than risking an intercepted pass, since it can kick for a field goal on fourth down.

■ THIRD AND SHORT (−2 YARDS)

Third and short, or third down and two or less yards to go, is almost always a running play, unless the team has completely lost confidence in its ability to run with the football. Remember, a running play should average about three yards and has a higher percentage of success than a passing play.

Third and short is considered the most critical situation from the defense's standpoint. The defense's ability to stop a short running play in this situation is in many ways a measure of its line and linebacker superiority.

Often, on third down and one yard to go, the defense will concede the first down while protecting against giving up big yardage by a trick pass. The defense reasons that it is highly unlikely that it will be able to stop a one-yard run unless it commits most of its personnel to the line of scrimmage, leaving virtually no pass protection.

■ FOURTH DOWN (AVERAGE OR WORSE FIELD POSITION)

What a team is likely to do on fourth-down situations depends on its field position. If it is in no better than average position (behind the opposing team's 40-yard line), it is out of field goal range. In this situation, you can expect a punt, with a try perhaps for a coffin corner kick that forces the opposition to accept the ball in poor field position behind its own 20-yard line.

In normal situations, you almost never will see the offense try to pick up the yardage needed for the first down when it is in average or worse field position, no matter how little yardage is needed. It is just too much of a gamble to risk giving up the football to the opposition in this field position — it is safer to move them back with the punt.

■ FOURTH DOWN (GOOD OR BETTER FIELD POSITION)

When the offense has moved beyond the defense's 40-yard line, it might be within field goal range, depending on the skills of its placekicker. In that case, expect a field goal try on fourth down.

The exception is when there are literally inches to go for a first down (and the coach likes to gamble), or when the team is so far behind that a field goal would do it no good at that point in the game. In such cases, you might see the offense use a blast or quarterback sneak to try to get the first down and continue the scoring drive. As a team's situation becomes more desperate, you can start to look for such bizarre offensive moves as the fake field goal and the fake punt.

We'll look at how time remaining and the score affect strategy in more detail in the next section.

Time Remaining and Score

The factors we've just considered — field position and down number and yards to go — are basic elements of percentage football, but they assume an abstract game in which the score is close. As an actual game progresses and one team assumes a lead, the score of the game and the time remaining become factors in themselves that affect strategy decisions.

As time runs out, you'll see the losing team start to take chances, primarily by passing the ball more. Although there are no hard-and-fast rules, you'll generally see teams starting to gamble in the situations listed in the chart at the right. When there are only two minutes left in the game, the entire style of play changes, as we'll see by looking at the two-minute drill.

Gambling Situations

BEGINNING OF SECOND HALF	BEHIND BY 28 OR MORE POINTS
BEGINNING OF FOURTH QUARTER	BEHIND BY 21 OR MORE POINTS
FIVE MINUTES REMAINING	BEHIND BY 14 OR MORE POINTS
TWO MINUTES REMAINING	BEHIND BY 7 OR MORE POINTS

■ THE TWO-MINUTE DRILL

When there are two minutes of playing time left at the end of each half, the referee so signals to both teams. After this 'two-minute warning', both teams, especially the offense, are likely to adjust their style of play.

If a team is in scoring position at the end of the first half, it might manipulate its play to get the most out of those two minutes. The clearest example of catchup football occurs, however, at the end of the game. The team that is ahead will try to consume as much time as possible, while the team that is behind tries to conserve time in an effort to score.

The offense usually has a set 'two-minute drill' designed to maximize its scoring chances which is practiced for just this occasion. As we'll see, it involves the use of time outs and plays that will stop the clock. Frequently, more than one play will be called in the huddle so the offense doesn't waste time between plays.

■ TIME OUTS

Each team is allowed three time outs per half. All teams try to save these three time outs for the two-minute drill so they can keep alive a scoring drive by calling time outs and stopping the clock. It is considered a mental error to use a time out prior to the two-minute warning.

Whether or not a team has time outs available can affect its game strategy. For example, suppose a team is behind by 3 points with ten seconds left in the game, and that it is on its opponent's 10-yard line. If it had just used its last time out, it would kick a field goal to tie the game and take its chances of winning the game in overtime. If it had one time out left, however, it could try one more quick play to score a touchdown and win the game, knowing that it could still call a time out and kick a field goal if that play failed.

■ STOPPING THE CLOCK

Since only three time outs are available per half, a team must devise other ways of stopping the clock. The rules provide that the clock stops following any incomplete pass, and for this reason you'll see a team resort to the passing game as time runs out.

If a pass is completed and the receiver is tackled on the field, the clock continues to run. On the other hand, if a ball carrier goes out of bounds with the ball in his possession, the clock stops. For this reason, sideline passes are an essential part of two-minute-drill strategy. If a receiver makes a catch and is about to be tackled, he will run out of bounds, stopping the clock. Some teams and quarterbacks are known for their ability to 'work the clock' during the two-minute drill.

(If the offense is ahead at the two-minute warning, it will attempt to keep possession with safe running plays. As time runs out, the quarterback will take the snap and simply fall to the ground, keeping the clock running.)

■ PREVENT DEFENSE

If the offense is behind and trying to catch up with its two-minute drill, you'll see the defense respond accordingly. It will try to keep the pass receivers in bounds and, in fact, often will leave the middle of the field open, hoping a receiver will catch a pass in this area and be tackled.

During the two-minute drill, you'll also see a winning defensive team put additional defensive backs into the game, in Nickel and Dime Defenses. It will allow short passes, protecting only the deep areas. This is known as a 'prevent' defense. The defense is willing to concede short passes in the middle of the field that keep the clock running and put its main defensive effort toward preventing the completion of a long bomb that could lead to a score.

(If the defense is behind, you'll see additional linemen and linebackers brought into the game in an attempt to force fumbles.)

■ THE KICKING GAME

Time remaining and score also affect kicking game strategy. Normally, a team will try for a field goal on fourth down if it is within range, rather than going for a first down in hopes of eventually scoring a touchdown. The theory is that it is better to put at least 3 points on the board than to gamble for 6 or 7. Near the end of the game, however, a team may be so far behind that a field goal is useless. Then you'll see it run or pass on fourth down, regardless of the yardage needed, to try and keep the scoring drive alive. On the other hand, if 3 points would win the game, you're likely to see a team try to 'stretch' the range of its field goal kicker on its final play.

If the team that is losing scores a touchdown during the last two minutes and is still behind, you'll probably see it try an onside kick in an attempt to keep possession of the ball.

Tendencies

Understanding percentage football enables a team to know that, ideally, its opponents should run, pass, punt, or try a field goal in a given field position and down number and yards-to-go situation. But, even if teams always played by the percentages (which they don't), this understanding still does not give any clue as to whether a run will be to the inside or outside, who will carry the football, whether a pass will be short, long, or medium, the type of pass routes to be run by the receivers, and who the most likely receiver might be. All of these factors are called 'team tendencies.'

A team studies game films of an upcoming opponent to try to spot such tendencies and to see how the opponent actually plays percentage football. A team also studies its own performance on game films, to find its own tendencies, as it knows the opposition is studying these films and will know its tendencies too.

■ RUN OR PASS

The first bit of data a team wants to know is the percentage of time its opponent will run and pass the ball in each situation. The team scouts its upcoming adversary and creates a chart which records each running or passing play according to the down number and yards-to-go situation. When the game is underway and the opposing team's offense goes into its huddle to call a play on, for example, first and ten in average field position, the defensive coach can look at his chart. If the statistics show that the offense runs eighty percent and play action passes twenty percent in this situation, the coach can gear his defense to the statistics.

The usefulness of any data, of course, depends on the judgment of both the person collecting it and the person interpreting it. A statistic that indicated a team passed eighty percent of the time in a particular situation could be misleading if one failed to take into account the fact that that team was behind in most of its games and therefore usually had to play catchup ball.

■ FORMATION

The teams look for further tip-offs as to whether the play will be a run or a pass. The formation is often a very important clue to this run/pass guessing game. Each team codes the formation used by its rival with regard to each situation and the type of play that results. It may find that a team runs out of the I Formation and Weak Side Set ninety percent of the time in a particular situation and play action passes ten percent, but that it play action passes ninety percent of the time if it comes out in a Strong Side Set in that situation. This would be an important refinement of the run vs. pass tendency statistics.

Obviously, these figures are only to illustrate how scouting for tendencies works. If possible, teams try to avoid such dramatic tendencies as the above, because they provide too great a clue to their opponents as to what they will do. However, since teams tend to do what they do well and avoid what they do poorly, the strengths and weaknesses of a team usually do produce such tendencies.

■ DIRECTION OF RUN

So far our scouting report has shown that a team can gather information on whether its opponent will run or pass on each down number and yards-to-go situation and for each field position and that it can further refine this information by finding the percent of time the team runs or passes out of various formations in that situation. Let's say that with this information the defense is about ninety percent sure that it is about to face a running play. The next question is: Where will the run go?

Each running play by a team is coded with regard to which of the ten running holes the play goes through. Once this information is gathered for several games, the defense can see the percentage of runs through each of these ten running holes overall, and for each field position, down, and formation situation. This information, of course, will influence the defense's gap and pursuit assignments.

■ BALL CARRIER, BLOCKING, AND FLOW

The defense also wants to know which running back will carry the ball. This essential piece of information is coded also and appears on the scouting report; it is helpful to the defense as it allows the linebackers to key on the usual ball carrier in a particular situation so they can get an additional jump on the play.

The team also codes whether the play was to the strong side or weak side, whether the play was with the blocking flow (as opposed to being a counter or misdirection play), and whether it was engineered with lead blocking or without.

Now a team can make a very good guess as to what the most likely plays will be when its opponent comes out of the offensive huddle and sets up in its formation. As the game progresses, if the opponent deviates from its prime tendencies (and, presumably, its highest percentage plays), the defense might assume that the opponent is frustrated or gambling.

■ DISTANCE OF PASS

We have looked at the information that a team gathers so it has a thorough understanding of its opponent's running game. Now let's look at how a team scouts its opponent's passing game.

The first information that is gathered is whether the team is likely to throw short, medium, or long in each game situation. Armed with this data, the defense can call its pass defense favoring either the short, medium, or long distance.

It might be interesting at this point to look back at the pass defense section to see examples of the many types of pass coverages the defense can throw at the offense. In general, zone coverages 'concede' the short pass while providing good protection against medium and long passes. Frequently, the defense will use some type of double coverage against the long pass. The defensive pass coverage call often is based on the tendency statistics.

■ ZONE, ROUTE, AND RECEIVER

The defense has an advantage if it knows whether the passing play in any situation is likely to be short, medium, or long, but it will have an additional advantage if it knows what percent of passes in a particular situation go to the various zones on the field. With this data the defense can lean toward more precise coverage of areas of the field that are favored by the offense's passing attack. If, for example, the defense were to find that on a third and long situation in average field position the offense liked to send two receivers to the deep middle zone, this obviously would be very helpful in organizing its pass defense call.

The defense also can code the types of pass routes run and the favored receivers. Let's say a team's scouting report shows that in a given situation the offense frequently tries a short pass to one of the two flat zones. There are five potential offensive receivers and they can run a variety of routes to end up in these zones. If the defense discovers that a certain receiver tends to run a certain route to the flat zone in this situation, it can call its defensive pass coverage accordingly. It will match up defensive with offensive personnel so that it has the best shot at forcing an incompletion or perhaps even gaining an interception.

Of course, as a spectator, you won't be able to keep track of all these tendencies the way the teams do. You'd need twenty clipboards, not to mention a small computer. However, if you're aware of how a team scouts its opponent, you're likely to spot some tendencies that will greatly increase your appreciation of the game.

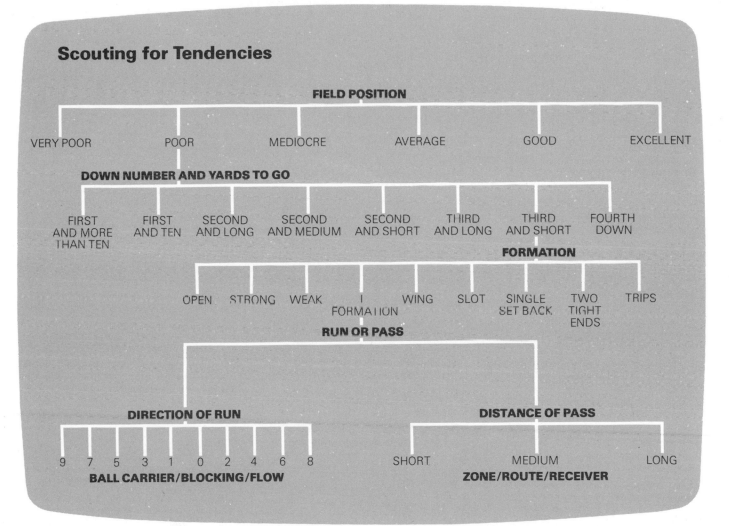

Scouting for Tendencies

FIELD POSITION

VERY POOR   POOR   MEDIOCRE   AVERAGE   GOOD   EXCELLENT

DOWN NUMBER AND YARDS TO GO

FIRST AND MORE THAN TEN   FIRST AND TEN   SECOND AND LONG   SECOND AND MEDIUM   SECOND AND SHORT   THIRD AND LONG   THIRD AND SHORT   FOURTH DOWN

FORMATION

OPEN   STRONG   WEAK   I FORMATION   WING   SLOT   SINGLE SET BACK   TWO TIGHT ENDS   TRIPS

RUN OR PASS

DIRECTION OF RUN

9   7   5   3   1   0   2   4   6   8

BALL CARRIER/BLOCKING/FLOW

DISTANCE OF PASS

SHORT   MEDIUM   LONG

ZONE/ROUTE/RECEIVER

SCOUTING THE DEFENSE

Scouting reports also focus on the defense, as the defensive coverage influences the type of play the offense calls and how it implements that play.

As you know from watching the defense in the Second Quarter, the defense first calls its pass defense, and this in turn dictates what the gap and pursuit assignments will be if the play turns out to be a run. For example, percentage football tells us that the offense is likely to run the ball on first and ten in average field position. The defense knows this and usually will call a strong safety zone rather than a cornerback zone pass defense so that the strong safety covers the short flat zone. Since the strong safety is a better tackler than the cornerback, this puts him up closer to the line of scrimmage so he can help out as a tackler on the presumed running play.

If the offense spots this type of coverage on first and ten, it may take advantage of it and try a play action pass to the flat zone, which would result in a mismatch of the slower strong safety covering the fleet flanker.

Teams keep track of defensive coverage during the game, as it helps the offensive play-calling. In order to accomplish this, it is important that the scouting coaches in the press box know in advance what the offensive play is going to be so they can scout how the defense covers it. This is one reason why it is considered undesirable to let a quarterback call his own plays. When the quarterback does call his own plays, only he knows what the play will be; the scouts in the press box must first pick up the offensive play and then try and see how the defense covers the play. When the coach calls the offensive play, he also can send this information to his scouting assistant coaches so that all they have to do is concentrate on the type of defense that is being used against their team's offensive play.

INDIVIDUAL TENDENCIES

The scouting report statistics tell much of the story, but not all of it. Ultimately, a team is made up of individual players, and it is the combined strengths and weaknesses of those players that produce overall team tendencies. In putting together a game strategy, a team must know as precisely as possible the strengths and weaknesses of its opponents, and those of its own players as well.

The players and coaches scout for individual tendencies by watching endless hours of game films. They watch these films in much the same way as we watched the individual players in the First and Second Quarters — position by position and move by move.

Does the quarterback pass better after dropping back or rolling out? Does he pass more accurately to the left or right? Do his fake handoffs really fool anybody? Which running back runs better to the inside and which to the outside? Which linemen block better to the left or right? What are the favorite pass routes of the wide receivers and the tight end? Which defensive lineman is the strongest rusher? Which linebacker makes the most quarterback sacks? Which secondary men are better at preventing or intercepting long or short passes? Which players are more effective playing zone or man-for-man? What areas of the zones do the defensive men tend to protect?

Finally, teams also look for subtle clues that might indicate what a player is apt to do during a particular play. These individual tendencies are referred to as 'tips'. From studying game films, a team might discover that a certain player may line up in a particular way for a certain play, or may have the nervous habit of opening and closing his fist if he is going to carry the football. Since these tips can give away a play, teams scout their own players for these individual tendencies and if they discover them, try to eliminate them.

Philosophies of Winning Football

We're going to conclude by looking at various philosophies, or systems, of football strategy. Some coaches try to initiate a balanced offensive attack, some prefer the security of the running game, and still others like to pass. There also is debate over how best to initiate a particular style of running or passing attack, as well as philosophical differences concerning defensive and special teams play.

As you watch a football game, you should be aware that, at the professional level (and even at some colleges), some coaches assume that they will have players talented enough to execute any philosophy; in other words, they develop their philosophy first and then recruit and train players and assistant coaches who will fit in with the 'system'. Other coaches acknowledge that any system has to be built around the individual skills of the players available.

■ OFFENSIVE BASE PLAYS

All coaches face the dilemma of wanting to have as many plays as possible, while having only limited practice time to make a given play effective. This dilemma usually is solved by adopting one or more 'base' plays.

A base play can be a running, passing, or even a kicking play. It is a play that the offense decides is going to be a bread-and-butter play for most normal situations. A base play might be any of the plays in our playbook — for example, a strong side off tackle play. (All the plays in the Third Quarter of this book are essentially base plays.)

Once a team decides on a base play, it has to perfect its execution. The offense must be able to block its base play so that it counters any possible defensive alignment and blocking scheme, including stunts and dogs. Much of the practice time on a base play is spent teaching the offense how to read different defensive moves so that the offense can use the appropriate blocking schemes to make the base play work.

■ PROTECTION PLAYS

If the defense is unsure whether the base play is coming its way, it will be easier for the offense to make the base play work, so the next step in developing a base play is to 'protect' it, by devising alternate plays that start out looking like the base play, but end up being another play. For example, if the base play is a run to the strong side, a play protecting the base play may be a counter play to the weak side, or it may be a play action pass. These protection plays may start from the same formation as the base play, or use an identical interior line blocking scheme, or have a running back following all or part of his assignment as on the base play. The possibility of a protection play prevents the defense from committing itself entirely, and this makes the base play more effective when it is executed.

The play or plays that protect the base play become, in effect, supplemental base plays.

THE PLAYBOOK

The game situation will not always lend itself to using the base play. For example, we already know that, in terms of percentage football, a team must pass on third down and long yardage to go on the 50-yard line. So, even if the team's base play is an off tackle play, nobody — including you, us, and the defense — expects it to run in this situation. The offense therefore must have a base play for this passing situation, must have alternative ways to block and run patterns for this base play, and must have plays that protect this passing base play.

Most teams develop several base plays for their playbooks, but the primary limitation on the number of plays is practice time. Most coaches consider it more important and more effective to perfect a few base plays, together with a repertoire of protection plays, than to strive for many radically different plays that can be given only minimum attention in practice.

How many base plays a team should have also is influenced by the sophistication of the defense of the opponents. The defense usually knows the offensive team's base play and practices stopping it with the same refinement that the offense practices executing it. Consequently, it is difficult to say exactly how many base plays a team should have. Practically speaking, the fewer the better — but enough to keep the defense guessing.

Finally, the playbook of a particular team usually will give some emphasis to either a running or a passing offense. Every team would like to have a balanced offense, but this is difficult to accomplish because to do so would mean to perfect both running and passing base plays for a variety of offensive situations. The teams that do emphasize one type of offense usually favor a running offense, using play action passes for the element of surprise and in passing situations. Other, but fewer, teams rely on a passing game to the point that they use running plays only for surprise.

OFF-BLOCKER RUNNING VS. OPTION RUNNING

We'll now look at some basic running and passing game philosophies. One running philosophy has the running back run 'off the block' of his teammates while pretty much ignoring the defense. This philosophy assigns a particular running hole for each play and directs the ball carrier through it. There is some leeway here, however. The running back is instructed to go through the hole by 'following the helmet' of his blocker; if his blocker's helmet is on the right side of the defensive man, he should run to the right side. In other words, the assigned running hole is not overly precise. Also, if there is no hole there because his blockers can't open one, the running back must do the best he can to find another way downfield. However, this running system is based on the offense acting as a unit, with the running backs having fairly strict assignments.

Under the other running philosophy, the running back carrying the ball is told, "The rest of the team is going to block for you — find the best hole and run through it." This is the basis of the 'option' running, or 'run to daylight', theory, but there are some constraints to it. If the play is to be run to the strong side off tackle hole, the ball carrier's choices usually would be holes that open up between his center and the strong side sideline. He is not expected to run to the opposite sideline. Also, the ball carrier does not run at random. He is taught to read how the defense is reacting to the blocking of his teammates so that he has the best chance of seeing the holes open up. But he does not run off his offensive blocking; he runs off the defense's reactions to these offensive blocks.

Which is best? The off-blocker running philosophy is more disciplined and depends more on the offensive blocking. The option running philosophy is more flexible and depends more on the skill of the running back. They both work.

■ STRAIGHT RUNNING VS. MIXED RUNNING

Running game philosophies also differ with regard to the types of plays used. The 'straight', or 'run at them', running philosophy assumes that the offensive line and running backs can surge forward up the middle play after play, each time picking up in excess of three yards per carry. If they can accomplish this, they will grind out first down after first down and march down the field for a touchdown. This approach also has been called the 'three yards and a cloud of dust' philosophy.

The 'mixed' running philosophy, on the other hand, bases its running attack on being unpredictable. This approach mixes up the running attack so that the defense always is guessing where the run will be aimed and how it will be executed. Misdirection plays and gadget or trick plays, such as reverses and double reverses, are staples of this philosophical diet.

■ PRIMARY PASS RECEIVER VS. QUARTERBACK READ

There also are various philosophies of the passing game. One passing philosophy designates a 'primary receiver' for each play and then manipulates the defense by using men in motion, alternate formations, and varied pass routes so that the primary receiver will be open. The quarterback expects to throw to that primary receiver, and he relies on the entire offensive scheme to make sure that receiver is free. The quarterback usually has a safety valve or secondary receiver to throw to if this system breaks down, however. This theory favors short passing plays.

The contrasting pass offense philosophy is the 'quarterback read' theory, which holds that all five eligible receivers are primary receivers and that it's up to the quarterback to read the entire field and find the open man. This theory relies on both the combination of pass routes and the individual skills of the receivers to make sure that one receiver will become free. Since defensive zone pass coverage forces the defense to play at least as deep as the deepest man in the zone, the pass routes are designed to create openings on the seams of the zones. This theory is designed to work best with medium passing plays using pass routes of about fifteen yards.

Which is best? The primary receiver theory is more disciplined (like the off-blocker running theory) and depends more on the system than on the skills of individual players. The quarterback read theory is more flexible (like the option running theory) and relies heavily on the quarterback's ability to read the defensive pass coverage as well as the talents of the pass receivers in eluding the defense.

Other passing theories fall in between these two. For example, the quarterback may decide, within the first two steps as he drops back after taking the snap from the center, to which side of the field he will throw and then to which of two or three receivers. Such a philosophy combines the two we have looked at. They all work.

■ BALL CONTROL PASSING VS. THE BOMB

Another type of passing philosophy concerns the strategic use of the short forward pass. The 'ball control' theory is based on short passes that can be thought of almost as running plays, with the short passes serving as long hand offs, without the ball carrier having to contend with the blocking of the defensive linemen. Such passes are relatively safe since there is little likelihood of an interception, particularly against zone coverage where the defenders play deeper than the receivers.

The 'bomb' passing philosophy takes the opposite tack. It threatens the defense with the possibility of the long touchdown pass at any time and from any place on the field. It depends on speedy receivers and a quarterback with a strong throwing arm. This philosophy is exciting and spectacular when it works, but usually it is low percentage football. When bombs are intercepted, however, the interceptions usually occur deep in the opponent's territory.

■ BASE DEFENSE VS. OPPONENT DEFENSE

There also are various defensive philosophies. One tries to devise basic defenses that work against any running or passing play, while the other tries to adjust the defensive plan for each game.

Because of practice-time limitations, it is preferable to come up with 'base' run and pass defenses that theoretically can counter any offense. The defense then can spend the entire season refining those base defenses. But is it really possible to devise a system that can cover all offensive contingencies?

The alternative is an 'opponent' defense theory that changes the defense for each game to challenge the base plays of each opponent. This theory must rely first on scouting the opponent so that its base plays are known, and then on devising defensive schemes to stop those plays. Can the defense practice a new system for each game and still be efficient? Teams have established successful defenses under both philosophies.

■ CONTAIN DEFENSE VS. FORCE DEFENSE

Defensive philosophies also break down into two main categories with regard to how they deal with the offensive running and passing games. Under one philosophy, the defense tries to 'contain' the offense. It plays conservatively against the running game, more or less allowing the very short one-, two-, and three-yard runs. The defense reasons that the offense eventually will make a mistake, such as missing an assignment or fumbling, and so will give up the ball through a turnover or by being forced to punt.

The passing game counterpart of the contain defensive philosophy usually assigns four men to rush, with the linebackers and secondary generally playing zone coverage. The defense tends to concede short passes and waits for the offense to make a mistake—especially hoping for the chance at an interception.

The alternative philosophy is based on the 'force', or 'penetrating', defense, which tries to make the offense make

mistakes. This defense uses stunts and dogs and other aggressive tactics against the running game, in an effort to force the offense into errors that will result in turnovers. Against the passing game, the force defense tends toward man-for-man coverage of the receivers and more blitzing by the linebackers and strong safety.

■ SPECIAL TEAMS PHILOSOPHY

The big question concerning special teams philosophy is the importance to give to this aspect of the game in terms of coaching and practice time. There is no debate as to its importance in the game itself—kicking is universally acknowledged to be one-third of the game. However, most teams work harder on perfecting their offense and defense than on special teams skills and are reluctant to use first-string personnel on special teams because of the risk of injuries. It is extremely rare for a college or pro team even to have an assistant coach whose only duty is to work with the special teams.

This is where we think the greatest change is being made in football. Coaches are beginning to feel that the special teams should receive more attention. To operate at full potential, the special teams must have base plays, blocking schemes for base plays, and alternative plays to protect base plays. We might see these in the seasons to come.

■ THE SYSTEM VS. THE INDIVIDUAL

Some coaches have earned reputations for following certain of these football philosophies. They devise a style of play, and then recruit players and assistant coaches who will be likely to carry it out. Frequently you'll hear that a new player is working on learning the team's 'system'. But what happens if the theoretical philosophy can't be carried out because of the human limitations of the people who must do the job?

An alternative approach recognizes that each individual player, no matter how talented, is able to do some things better than others. The task for the coach is to utilize the strengths and avoid the weaknesses of each player, adding up to a team of players who do what they do best. A coach who thinks this way will also tend to deal with his opponents in similar fashion. He will pit his team's strengths against his opponents' weaknesses, even if that means altering his philosophy game by game.

Eventually, a coach who bases his philosophy on the individual skills of his players may got the reputation for having a distinct offensive or defensive style. In actuality, however, he merely utilized his personnel efficiently and, by doing so, a style of sorts developed.

■ PHYSICAL VS. MENTAL SKILLS

Finally, there is debate within football concerning the responsibility of each player to play his position. Ultimately, it is the play at the individual level that makes or breaks any team's philosophy. But which football skills are more important physical or mental? The consensus is, as you might expect, that both are.

It certainly is crucial that each man at each position physically dominate his opponent for a given play to work; however, dominance in football is an art. Brute strength and toughness are not enough. A skilled, intelligent player will have a great advantage over one who has only courage under his helmet.

So, as you watch the game, realize that the popular notion that football is solely a physical contest is only half the story. Physical attributes and conditioning are important, to be sure, but the ability to be a winning football player must be learned and practiced.

FLAG DOWN

Officials, Rules, and Penalties

When you hear an official blow his whistle or see him toss a yellow flag on the field and make a signal, it's time for the enforcement of one or more of the many rules of football. This section has been prepared to help you understand those rules and the penalties for violating them. It is based on the rules of the National Football League for the 1980 pro season.

It is important to keep in mind that what follows are not all the rules of the game, or the exact wording of the rules. The official rulebook is more than a hundred pages in length and reads like the Internal Revenue Code. There are many exceptions to the rules not covered here and some rules that we have left out.

What follows are what we consider to be the more important and/or interesting rules of the game. We'll start by looking at specific rules and the signals and penalties associated with them. Then we'll look at the officials and their duties. At the end of this section, we'll make note of some of the major ways in which the rules of college and Canadian football differ from those of the National Football League.

■ THE FIELD AND THE FOOTBALL

Dimensions. The playing portion of the field is 360 feet long, including the two end zones, and 160 feet wide. There is a white border, 6 feet wide, that rims the sidelines and end lines. The goal line is 8 inches wide.

There are 'hash marks' on each side of the field which are 70 feet, 9 inches from each sideline. At the conclusion of a play, if the ball is downed outside of those hash marks, it is moved to the nearest hash mark for the start of the next play; if the ball is downed in between the hash marks, it stays where it is. This keeps the ball and thus the play of the game toward the middle of the field.

The line used to spot the ball for the extra-point try is two yards from the goal line.

Out of Bounds. The sidelines and end lines (including the white border) are out of bounds. The goal line marking itself is in the end zone.

Goal Posts. The goal posts must be painted bright gold and must be of the single standard type, padded at the

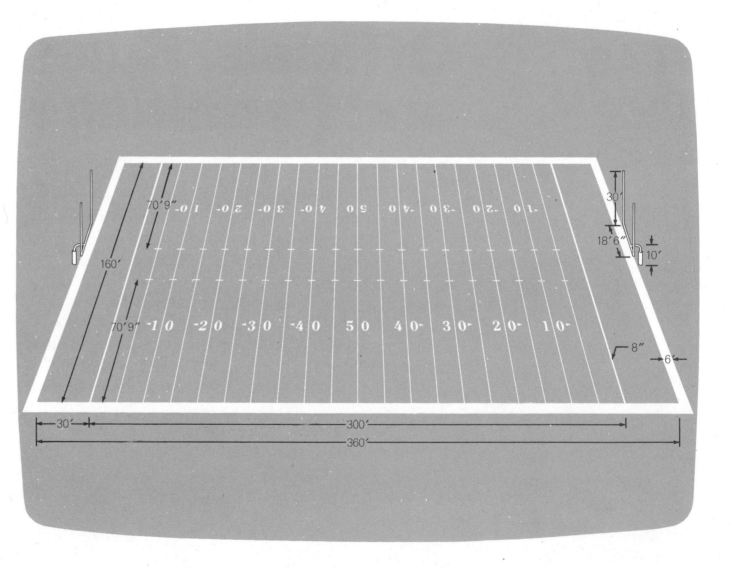

hase, and offset from the end lines. The crossbar is 18 feet, 6 inches wide, with the top of the crossbar 10 feet above the ground. The vertical posts must be between 3 and 4 inches in diameter and must rise at least 30 feet above the crossbar, with a 42-inch ribbon attached to the top of each post

Markings and Field Decorations. Pylons must be used to mark the intersections of the sideline and end zone markings and the corners of the end zones. All field markings, including yard-line numbers, are standardized.

Field decorations, such as the football team's insignia painted in the end zone or at the 50-yard line, must be approved by the Commissioner of Football so that they will not cause any confusion with other markings on the field.

The Football. The regulation football must be a 'Wilson', hand selected, bearing the signature of the Commissioner. Its case is made of tan, pebble-grained leather. Its shape is a 'prolate spheroid', 11 to 11¼ inches on the long axis, 28 to

28½ inches on the long circumference, and 21¼ to 21½ inches on the short circumference. It may weigh 14 to 15 ounces.

The home team must have twenty-four footballs ready to be checked by the referee at least one hour before game time. The offensive team captain can request a new football during bad weather conditions.

■ **THE PLAYERS AND THEIR EQUIPMENT**

Number of Players. Each team may play with no more than eleven players. There is no penalty for playing with less than eleven players.

Penalty: more than eleven players on field, 5 yards.

Substitutions. Unlimited substitution is permitted, but players may enter the field only when the ball is dead. The player substituted for must leave the field

on his team's sideline before the snap. Once a player has entered the field and communicated with one of his team-mates on the field, he must remain in the game for at least one play.

Penalties: illegally entering field, 15 yards; illegal substitution or return, 5 yards.

Equipment. All players must wear helmets with chin straps fastened; shoulder, hip, thigh, and knee pads; and shoes and stockings. Kicking shoes must be standard and cannot be modified. (Barefoot kicking is permitted.) Tearaway jerseys are illegal.

Players may not wear equipment that, in the opinion of the officials, endangers other players, including projecting hard plates, guards, or protective devices, unless they are covered with foam rubber. Casts, tape, or bandages on the hand or wrist may be used only to protect an injury and must be permitted by the umpire. Players may not wear sharp shoe cleats and may not use grease or slippery substances on their equipment, person, or clothing.

All players on a team must wear uniforms of the same color. The visiting team must wear jerseys that are not similar in color to those of the home team. Uniforms may not be so similar to the color of the ball as to be confusing.

Penalty: illegal equipment, suspension from succeeding play.

Numbering. All players must have numbers on their jerseys that correspond to their positions, as follows: quarterbacks and kickers, 1 to 19; running backs and defensive backs, 20 to 49; centers and linebackers, 50 to 59; offensive linemen (including centers), 60 to 79; defensive linemen, 60 to 79 and 90 to 99; wide receivers and tight ends, 80 to 89.

A player entering the game who does not play in a position consistent with the above numbering system must report this to the referee.

Penalty: failure to notify referee of eligibility change, 5 yards.

NO TIME OUT
OR
TIME IN WITH WHISTLE

TIME OUT

REFEREE'S TIME OUT
(FOLLOWING TIME OUT SIGNAL)

DELAY OF GAME
OR
EXCESS TIME OUT

■ TIMING THE GAME

Periods. A game is sixty minutes long, divided into four periods, or quarters, of fifteen minutes each. There is a two-minute intermission between the first and second quarters and the third and fourth quarters. The intermission between the second and third quarters (halftime) is fifteen minutes.

Coin Toss. Three minutes before the kickoff, the coin toss takes place in the middle of the football field. The referee tosses the coin, and the visiting team captain calls heads or tails. The winner of the coin toss may choose either: (1) to kick or receive, or (2) the goal his team will defend. The loser gets the option that has not been chosen.

Between the first and second and the third and fourth quarters, the teams change sides of the field.

At the end of the first half, both team captains go to the center of the field to inform the referee of their choice for the beginning of the second half. The team captain who lost the coin toss at the beginning of the game gets to choose first from the same two options.

Penalty: delay of start of half, 15 yards from spot of kickoff and loss of coin toss option.

The Clock. The stadium clock is the official clock of the game. If the stadium clock malfunctions, the line judge continues to time the game until the clock is again operational.

The clock starts when the ball is kicked off to start the game. The clock stops when: (1) the ball goes out of bounds, (2) a pass is incomplete, (3) the quarterback is sacked behind the line, (4) at the end of a down when a foul occurs, (5) the ball is downed across the goal line for a score, (6) after a fair catch, (7) upon a change of possession by the teams, and (8) when a team or the referee calls a time out.

When the clock is stopped for any of the above reasons, it starts again when the ball is next snapped or kicked off. (After a quarterback sack, the referee's whistle starts the clock.)

Time Outs. The referee may call time outs for an injury to a player, to measure for a first down, or for various other reasons within his discretion to preserve playing time.

Each team may call three time outs during each half. On each of these team time outs, the field judge starts his stopwatch, then blows his whistle after one minute and thirty seconds to indicate that play will begin.

Penalty: excess team time outs, 5 yards.

Delay of Game. The team in possession of the ball has thirty seconds after the end of a play to put the ball back in play. This time is displayed on two 30-second clocks on the field and visible to the players. If this thirty-second limit is exceeded, the field judge calls a delay-of-game penalty.

Other acts by a team to consume or conserve playing time that constitute delay of the game include: failing to assemble promptly for the next play, remaining on a dead ball or downed runner, attempts by a runner to advance after his progress has been stopped ('crawling'), and actions that prevent the referee from promptly starting the next play.

Penalties: delay of game, crawling, or attempts to consume or conserve time, 5 yards.

Two-Minute Warning. When there are two minutes remaining in each half, the referee so signals. Thereafter, special rules apply to timing the game.

While the clock usually starts with the kickoff, in the final two minutes of a half, if there is a kickoff, the clock does not start until the ball is legally touched by any player on the field of play.

A fourth time out is allowed without penalty for any injured player. Additional time outs are allowed for further injuries, but a penalty is assessed against the injured team if the clock was running when the player was injured. The team awarded any of these extra injury time outs may not put the ball in play for at least ten seconds, and the half or the game can end while these ten seconds are being run off the clock.

Finally, a team cannot stop the clock by deliberately trying to get a penalty.

End of Game. If time expires while the ball is in play, time is not called until that down ends. During such a down, a foul by the defense can extend the game by one down at the option of the offense, but a foul by the offense does not extend the game.

If a touchdown is made on the last play of the game, the try for the extra point is permitted.

Overtime. When the score is tied at the end of the regulation playing time, the referee repeats the coin toss just as he did at the beginning of the game. Following a three-minute intermission, play continues for fifteen minutes. The first team that scores by any means wins the game. Each team has two time outs for this period. The rules governing the two-minute-warning period apply.

A pre-season or regular season game that ends in a tie after this fifteen-minute overtime period remains a tie. In playoff games, however, this overtime procedure continues until either team scores.

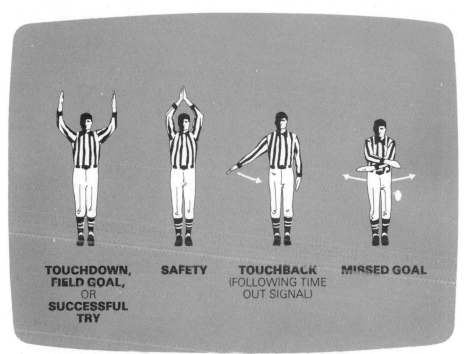

TOUCHDOWN, FIELD GOAL, OR SUCCESSFUL TRY **SAFETY** **TOUCHBACK** (FOLLOWING TIME OUT SIGNAL) **MISSED GOAL**

■ SCORING THE GAME

Touchdown. A touchdown is scored when any part of the ball which is legally in the possession of an in-bounds player is on, above, or over the opposing team's goal line (unless it is ruled a touchback). A team that scores a touchdown is awarded 6 points.

Extra-Point Try. After a team has scored a touchdown, it can try for one extra point on one more down. That team can have the ball placed anywhere between the in-bounds lines and two yards from the goal line. To gain this extra point, the team may placekick or drop kick the ball through the goal post uprights, or it may try to run or complete a pass across the goal line.

The extra-point try is for this one extra point only. The defense, for example, cannot score on an extra-point try. The ball is dead if the kick is blocked or the defense gets possession of the ball.

If a foul by the defense during the extra-point try prevents the try from being attempted, the down is replayed.

Field Goal. A field goal is scored by the offensive team placekicking (or drop kicking) the ball so that the entire ball passes above the crossbar and between the uprights of the goal post, or through a vertical plane that extends indefinitely above the crossbar and the outside edges of the uprights. A field goal counts for 3 points.

If a field goal is attempted and missed on a down when the line of scrimmage is outside the 20-yard line, the defense takes over the ball at that line of scrimmage. If the missed attempt is from a line of scrimmage inside the 20-yard line, the defense takes over on its 20-yard line.

If a field goal is successful, the team scored upon has the option of either kicking off or receiving a kickoff.

Safety. Two points are awarded the defensive team if the ball is ruled dead on or behind the offensive team's goal line, but only if it was the 'impetus' (action of the offensive team that gave momentum to the ball) that caused the ball to become dead. For example, if a quarterback retreats into his own end zone, as in dropping back to throw a pass, and then is tackled, it was the impetus of the quarterback that brought the ball into the end zone, so it counts as a safety.

It is a safety, too, if a blocked punt goes into the kicking team's end zone, or if a receiving team's player muffs a punt and forces it into his end zone, where he or a teammate recovers it. Likewise, if the offensive team commits a foul and the spot of enforcement is behind its goal line.

It is not a safety, however, if a defensive player intercepts a pass in his own end zone and is downed there, or if he intercepts a pass within his own 5-yard line and his momentum carries him into his end zone. A ball passed from behind the offensive team's goal line that is batted down is an incomplete pass, not a safety.

After a safety, the team *scored upon* puts the ball in play from its own 20-yard line by placekicking, drop kicking, or punting.

FIRST DOWN   **FOURTH DOWN**   **LOSS OF DOWN**

Touchback. A touchback occurs when the ball is declared dead on or behind a team's own goal line and the impetus came from the opposing team (provided it is not a touchdown or missed field goal by the opposing team). The most common situation is a kickoff or punt that goes into the receiving team's end zone.

A touchback does not count for any score; the ball is spotted from the end zone up to the 20-yard line for the start of play.

■ DOWNS

Series of Downs. A down is a period of action that starts with the ball being put in play and ends with the ball being declared dead. The offensive team must advance the ball ten yards in four consecutive downs from scrimmage in order to retain possession of the football.

If a series of downs starts inside the defense's 10-yard line, the offense has four downs to score a touchdown or field goal.

First Down. A new series of downs, or first down, starts when the offense advances the ball beyond the necessary ten-yard distance. If the offense fails to do so, the ball is awarded to the defensive team for a new series of downs, starting where the ball was declared dead at the end of the offensive fourth down. The forward part of the ball, where dead, is the determining point in measuring for a first down.

If possession of the ball changes during a play, it is a first down for the team in possession at the end of the play. On a kick from scrimmage (described below) it is a first down for the kicking team if it recovers the kick after it had been first touched by the receiving team.

Fouls. When a penalty for a foul is enforced against the offense, the down number for the next play remains the same as it was for the play in which the foul was committed. A foul by the defense usually results in a first down for the offense, in addition to any penalty yardage. (Exceptions are described in the section below on 'Enforcement of Penalties'.)

■ FORMATIONS AND OFFSIDE

Line of Scrimmage. There is a neutral zone or space, the length of the football, that stretches across the field where the ball is spotted for play. The line of scrimmage for the offensive and defensive teams is considered to be at their respective points of the football, with the neutral zone in between. No player may violate this neutral zone (except the center when he assumes his position to snap the ball).

Offensive Formation. The offensive formation must have at least seven players with their hands, feet, or heads within one foot of their line of scrimmage. Those players not on the line must be at least one yard behind the line at the snap of the ball (except for the quarterback). Linemen may lock their legs only with the player snapping the ball. No player may be out of bounds at the snap.

Penalties: illegal snap formation, or out of bounds at snap, 5 yards.

Motion and Shifts. All offensive players (except one backfield man) must

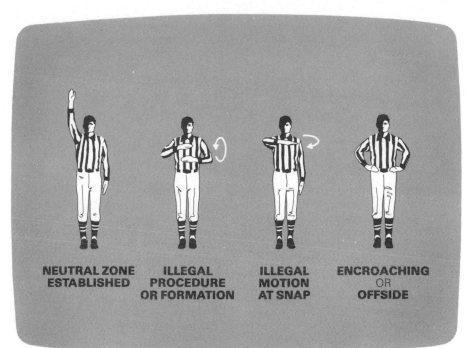

NEUTRAL ZONE ESTABLISHED   ILLEGAL PROCEDURE OR FORMATION   ILLEGAL MOTION AT SNAP   ENCROACHING OR OFFSIDE

come to a complete stop, or set position, for at least one second before the snap, without any movement. At the snap, all offensive players must be stationary, except for one back, who may be in motion parallel to the line of scrimmage, or backward, but not forward. Once assuming a set position, no offensive player may move in such a way as to make the defense think that the snap has started.

No interior lineman may move after taking a three-point stance. Other offensive players may shift at the same time from one set position to another before the snap, provided they come to a one-second stop as described above.

The offense may not 'double shift' on or inside its opponent's 20-yard line, unless that double shift has occurred outside the 20-yard line at least three times previously in the game.

Penalties: false start, illegal motion or shift, or illegal pause after shift, 5 yards.

Defensive Alignment. There are no restrictions on the way the defensive players may align themselves, or on their motion before the snap, so long as they do not violate the neutral zone or touch the snapper.

Penalty: interference with the snap, 5 yards.

Encroachment and Offside. A player may charge into the neutral zone and retreat from it before the ball is snapped without penalty, provided he does not make contact with an opponent or draw an opponent opposite him into an encroachment or offside violation, and provided that his charging into the neutral zone is not a repeated act.

A player is offside if any part of his body is beyond his line of scrimmage when the ball is snapped.

Penalty: encroachment or being offside, 5 yards.

The Snap. The offense must put the ball in play by a snap from the line of scrimmage (unless a free kick is provided for). The snap must start with the ball on the ground with its long axis at right angles to the line. The snap must be made with one quick and continuous motion, and the ball must actually leave or be taken from the snapper's hands. The snapper may not slide his hands along the ball before grasping it and may not move his feet until the ball has left his hands. The snap must be to a player who was not on the line at the snap.

Penalties: illegal snap or snap to ineligible receiver, 5 yards.

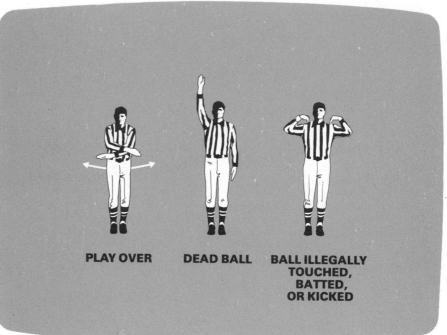

PLAY OVER   DEAD BALL   BALL ILLEGALLY TOUCHED, BATTED, OR KICKED

■ POSSESSION OF THE BALL

Fumbles and Muffs. A 'fumble' is the loss of possession of the ball by a player. A 'muff' is the touching of a loose ball by a player in an unsuccessful attempt to gain possession of the ball. The distinction is that the term 'fumble' always implies possession.

Advancing the Ball. A fumble may be recovered and advanced by any player on either team, regardless of whether it is recovered before or after

it hits the ground. When a fumble is recovered simultaneously by two opposing players, possession is awarded to the team that made the fumble.

If a ball carrier intentionally fumbles forward, it is considered a forward pass.

On fourth down, if a fumble occurs during a play from scrimmage, the player who fumbled is the only offensive player who may recover and advance the ball. If any other offensive player recovers, the ball is next snapped from the spot of the fumble, or the spot of recovery if it is behind the spot of the fumble. A fourth-down fumble that rolls out of bounds is likewise put in play from the spot of the fumble or the out-of-bounds spot, whichever is further back. The same rules apply during the two-minute-warning period, regardless of the down number.

Batting the Ball. It is illegal to bat or punch a loose ball toward the opponent's goal line while it is in the field of play, or in any direction while in the end zone.

A pass in flight may not be batted by the offense toward the opponent's goal line, but any pass (forward or backward) may be batted in any direction by the defense.

No player may deliberately kick at the ball except as a placekick, drop kick, or punt.

Penalties: illegally batting, punching, or kicking the ball, 15 yards.

Dead Ball. The ball is declared dead and the down ended when: (1) a runner is held or restrained so that his forward progress is stopped, (2) a runner is contacted by a defensive player so that it causes the runner to touch the ground with any part of his body other than his hands or feet, (3) a runner goes out of bounds, and (4) on an incomplete forward pass. Other situations that result in the ball being declared dead are discussed below.

When the ball is declared dead, it is usually put in play at the spot where it was declared dead.

Ball Out of Bounds. If a runner goes out of bounds, the ball is put in play at the out-of-bounds spot. If a forward pass goes out of bounds, the ball is put in play at the previous spot of the ball (plus loss-of-down penalty). If a backward pass or a fumble goes out of bounds, the ball is put in play at the out-of-bounds spot by the team last in possession.

The rules regarding out-of-bounds kicks are discussed below under 'The Kicking Game'.

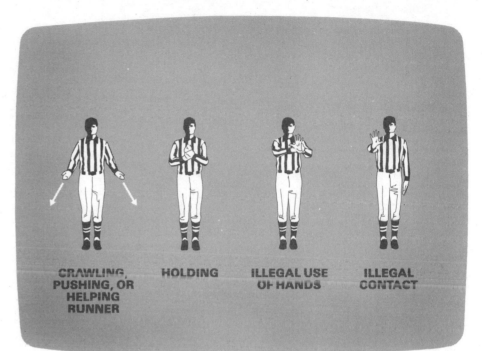

CRAWLING, PUSHING, OR HELPING RUNNER   HOLDING   ILLEGAL USE OF HANDS   ILLEGAL CONTACT

■ BLOCKING AND TACKLING

Offensive Blocking. Offensive run blocking is aggressive action by a blocker to obstruct an opponent from the ball carrier. An offensive blocker can assist a runner only by blocking for him. Players may not push or lift the runner or interlock with each other to block.

The ball carrier may use his hands and arms to ward off tacklers, but no other offensive player may use his hands, arms, or legs to grasp, hang onto, encircle, push from behind, or trip an opponent to gain an advantage. Hands with arms extended cannot be used to contact an opponent either inside or outside his frame.

During a legal pass protection block, hands may be thrust forward, either open or closed, but they must be kept inside the blocker's elbows, and may contact a defensive player only within his frame. Hands may not be used to contact an opponent on the neck, face, or head. An offensive blocker may use an

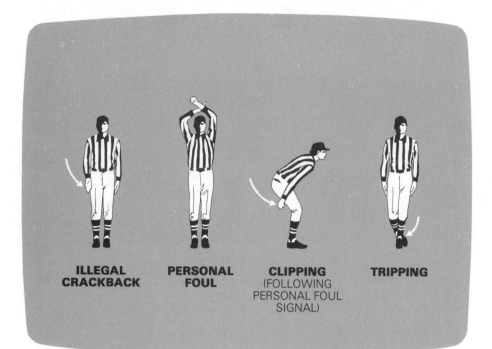

ILLEGAL CRACKBACK   **PERSONAL FOUL**   **CLIPPING** (FOLLOWING PERSONAL FOUL SIGNAL)   **TRIPPING**

up-and-down motion of his arms to ward of an opponent's attempt to grab his jersey or arms, or contact his head.

Penalties: assisting runner, holding, or illegal use of hands, arms, or body by offense, 10 yards.

Crackback Block. An offensive player who lines up more than two yards outside his tackle may not 'clip' (see below) an opponent anywhere, nor may he contact him below the waist if the defensive man is moving toward the ball

and contact is made within five yards on either side of the line of scrimmage.

Penalty: illegal crackback block, 15 yards.

Defensive Blocking. A defensive player may not tackle or hold any opponent other than a ball carrier or an offensive player who pretends to be a ball carrier.

A defensive player may use his hands, arms, or body to defend or protect himself from an obstructing opponent, to push or pull an opponent out of the way

on the line of scrimmage, in an attempt to tackle a runner or recover a loose ball, or in a legal block.

Eligible pass receivers may be blocked below the waist only if they are lined up within two yards of the offensive tackles, at or behind the line of scrimmage. Defensive players may contact eligible receivers (wherever lined up) to obstruct them only within five yards beyond the line of scrimmage, and only if such contact is continuous and unbroken. A defensive player may not use his hands or arms to push from behind, hang onto, or encircle an eligible receiver so as to restrict his movement as the play develops.

A defensive player may not contact an opponent above the shoulders with the palm of his hand, except to ward him off the line, or in a legal attempt to get at the ball.

Penalties: illegal use of hands, arms, or body by defense, 5 yards (and first and ten for offense).

Clipping. No player may throw his body across the back of the leg or into the back of an opponent after approaching him from behind, unless the player is a ball carrier or the act occurs in the area between the tackles and three yards on either side of the line of scrimmage.

Penalty: clipping, 15 yards.

Personal Fouls. All players are prohibited from butting with the helmet, striking with the fists, kicking or kneeing, striking on the head with the heel, back, or side of the hand, wrist, forearm, or elbow, striking with the elbow or forearm by swinging the body, grasping a face mask, piling on, tackling a runner out of bounds or a player obviously out of the play, or engaging in unnecessary roughness.

Penalties: personal fouls, first down (if by defense) and 15 yards (and disqualification if flagrant).

Passing and Kicking Fouls. Special rules regarding blocking and personal fouls are discussed in the sections below on 'The Passing Game' and 'The Kicking Game'.

ILLEGAL FORWARD PASS **INCOMPLETE PASS** **PASS JUGGLED IN BOUNDS AND CAUGHT OUT OF BOUNDS** **INELIGIBLE RECEIVER DOWNFIELD**

TOUCHING A FORWARD PASS **INTERFERENCE WITH FORWARD PASS** **INTENTIONAL GROUNDING OF PASS** **RUNNING INTO PASSER (FOLLOWING PERSONAL FOUL SIGNAL)**

■ THE PASSING GAME

Forward Pass. The offensive team may attempt only one forward pass during each play from scrimmage. A forward pass may not be thrown once the ball has crossed the line of scrimmage, and the passer must be behind his line of scrimmage when the pass is thrown. The pass begins when the passer brings his hand forward to throw the football. If the ball comes loose after the passer's hand has moved forward, it is an incomplete pass; if the ball comes loose before this, it is a fumble.

Penalties: forward pass not from scrimmage, 5 yards from spot of pass; second forward pass behind line, loss of down from previous spot; forward pass from beyond the line, loss of down and 5 yards from spot of pass.

Completed Passes. In order for a pass to be complete, an eligible receiver must touch the field with both feet in bounds while in possession of the football. If the receiver is in possession in the air and is carried out of bounds by a defender, the pass is complete at that out-of-bounds spot. If an eligible receiver goes out of bounds or is forced out of bounds and then comes back in bounds to catch a pass, the pass is ruled incomplete.

A forward pass is incomplete and the ball is ruled dead if it hits the ground, goes out of bounds, hits the goal post or crossbar, is caught by an offensive player after touching an ineligible receiver, or is an illegal pass caught by an offensive player. If a forward pass is caught simultaneously by an eligible offensive player and a defensive man, possession goes to the passing team.

Penalty: incomplete pass, loss of down.

Eligible Receivers. A forward pass may not be touched or caught by anyone but an eligible receiver. All members of the defensive team are eligible receivers, but the only eligible receivers on the offensive team are the players on either farthest end of the line and the players who are at least one yard behind the line of scrimmage at the snap of the ball.

All offensive players become eligible to catch a pass once the pass is touched by any eligible receiver. If the offensive team lines up in a T Formation, the quarterback is not an eligible receiver if he receives the snap.

Ineligible receivers may not advance beyond the line of scrimmage before the ball leaves the passer's hands, and no offensive player may block beyond the line (except for the initial charge of linemen) from the time of the snap until the pass is touched by a player of either team. Either of such acts is considered pass interference.

Penalties: unintentional touching of ball by ineligible receiver, loss of down; intentional touching of ball by ineligible receiver, loss of down and 10 yards from previous spot.

Pass Interference. Both offensive and defensive players have a right to the path of the football. It is pass interference when any player's movement beyond the line of scrimmage hinders the progress of any eligible receiver (offensive or defensive) in his attempt to reach the pass. This rule applies to the offensive team when the ball is snapped and to the defensive team when the ball leaves the passer's hands.

When two or more players make incidental contact in a simultaneous and bona fide attempt to catch or bat away the ball, there is no pass interference, even if such contact is severe.

Penalties: pass interference by offense, 10 yards from previous spot; pass interference by defense, first down at spot of foul (and distance penalty if personal foul).

Intentional Grounding. Intentional grounding of a forward pass is not permitted. This occurs when the ball hits the ground after it has been thrown, tossed, or lobbed by the passer in an

effort to prevent a loss of yardage by his team.

Penalty: intentional grounding, loss of down and 10 yards from previous spot (safety, if passer in end zone).

Roughing the Passer. A defensive player is not allowed to run into the passer after the ball has left his hand if that defensive player has a reasonable chance to stop his momentum in his attempt to block the pass or tackle the passer.

Penalty: running into or roughing the passer, first down and 15 yards from previous spot (and disqualification if flagrant).

Backward Pass. Any pass other than a forward pass is considered a backward pass or a lateral; a pass parallel to the line of scrimmage is also a backward pass. A ball carrier always may backward pass or lateral the football, and any offensive or defensive player may recover it either in the air or after it has hit the ground. A lateral or backward pass

that hits the ground and is recovered by an offensive man can be advanced, but such a pass can only be recovered (not advanced) by the defensive team. A backward pass that is caught in the air can be advanced by the defensive team.

Enforcement of Passing Penalties. If a personal foul is commited by the offense prior to a pass being completed, the penalty is assessed from the previous line of scrimmage. In the case of a personal foul being committted by a defensive player prior to a pass being completed, the penalty is assessed from the spot where the ball becomes dead.

If defensive pass interference occurs in the defensive team's end zone, it is a first down for the offense on the defense's 1-yard line, or half the distance to the goal if the previous spot was within the 1-yard line.

If, on a fourth-down play, the offense throws an incomplete pass from within twenty yards of the defense's goal line, the defense takes possession at its own 20-yard line.

FREE KICK VIOLATION

INELIGIBLE MEMBER OF KICKING TEAM DOWNFIELD

TOUCHING A SCRIMMAGE KICK

ROUGHING KICKER (FOLLOWING PERSONAL FOUL SIGNAL)

BLOCKING BELOW THE WAIST

INTERFERENCE WITH FAIR CATCH

INVALID FAIR CATCH SIGNAL (FOLLOWING INTERFERENCE WITH FAIR CATCH SIGNAL)

■ THE KICKING GAME

Types of Kick. There are three types of kick. On a 'placekick', the ball is kicked from a fixed position on the ground. It may be held by a teammate, supported in a depression in the ground, or, on the kickoff, supported by an artificial kicking tee.

A 'drop kick' is made by the kicker dropping the ball and kicking it immediately after it touches the ground. (It is rarely used in football today.)

A 'punt' is made by the kicker dropping the ball and kicking it before the ball hits the ground.

Kickoff. The kickoff is one situation in which the kicking team has a 'free kick', meaning that the opposing team cannot interfere with the kicker. The kickoff may be made by a placekick or drop kick, but not by a punt. It is permissible to placekick the kickoff from a kicking tee.

The kickoff is made at the start of each half and after a field goal and extra-point try following a touchdown. The ball is spotted on the kicking team's 35-yard line.

To be legal, a kickoff must travel at least ten yards or be touched by a member of the receiving team. A legal free kick may be recovered by the receiving team and advanced; the kicking team may recover a legal kick but may not advance the ball (unless a member of

the receiving team had possession of the ball and lost possession).

When a kickoff goes out of bounds on the sideline between the two goal lines without being touched by a member of the receiving team, it must be kicked again. An out-of-bounds kickoff that was first touched by the receiving team is the receivers' ball at the out-of-bounds spot.

If a kickoff goes out of bounds behind the receivers' goal line, is downed in the end zone, or strikes the receivers' goal post, it is a touchback; the ball is spotted for the receiving team at its 20-yard line. A kickoff that goes through the uprights on the goal post is not a field goal.

Penalties: illegal free kick formation, illegal free kick, short free kick, illegally out of bounds on free kick, or illegal touching of free kick by offense, 5 yards and rekick.

Safety Kick and Fair-Catch Kick. There are two other situations in which a team may free kick. After a safety, the team *scored upon* puts the ball in play by a free kick from its own 20-yard line. After a 'fair catch' (see below), the team that made the catch may free kick from the mark of the catch.

Safety and fair-catch kicks may be by placekick, drop kick, or punt, but no kicking tee may be used. A field goal may be scored on a fair-catch kick, but not on a safety kick.

Scrimmage Kicks. A 'kick from scrimmage' is a situation where the kicking team kicks after putting the ball in play by a snap, and in which the defense may try to oppose the kicker. A team may kick from scrimmage on any down, and may punt, drop kick, or placekick. (A scrimmage kick by a team on fourth down is commonly called a 'punt' because this method of kicking virtually always is used. The other scrimmage kick situations are the field goal and the extra-point try, which are discussed in the section on 'Scoring the Game'. Only a placekick or drop kick may be used to try for a field goal or to kick an extra point.)

During a kick from scrimmage, only the two end men in the kicking team formation (whether on the line or in the backfield) may advance beyond the line before the ball is kicked.

The receiving team may recover and advance any punt or unsuccessful field goal try, whether or not it crosses its goal line and whether such recovery is beyond or behind the line of scrimmage. A punt

or missed field goal that touches a goal post is dead.

The kicking team may never advance a scrimmage kick that goes beyond the line of scrimmage. If a member of the kicking team touches the ball before it is touched by the receiving team, it is first and ten for the receiving team at the point of touching. If a kicking-team member recovers the kick after it has been touched by the receiving team, it is first and ten for the kicking team at the point of recovery. No member of the kicking team who has been out of bounds may touch or recover the ball until after it has been touched by the receiving team.

A punt that is blocked and does not cross the line of scrimmage may be recovered by either team; however, if the kicking team recovers a punt made on fourth down, it must make the yardage necessary for a first down to retain possession.

Penalties: leaving the line before ball is kicked, or kicking team player out of bounds, 5 yards; illegal touching of

scrimmage kick, receivers' ball at spot of illegal touching.

Field Goal and Extra Point. Rules pertaining to the field goal and extra-point try are discussed in the section on 'Scoring the Game'.

Roughing the Kicker. A member of the receiving team may not run into or rough a kicker who kicks behind his line of scrimmage unless the contact was incidental to and after he had touched the ball in flight, was caused by the kicker's own motions, or occurred during a 'quick' kick (not out of kicking formation) or after the kicker had recovered a loose ball.

Penalties: running into the kicker, 5 yards; roughing the kicker, 15 yards (and disqualification if flagrant).

Blocking on Kicking Plays. All players on the receiving team are prohibited from blocking below the waist on a free kick or scrimmage kick, except that, on a kick from scrimmage, players lined up within two yards of the tackles may be blocked below the waist at or *behind* the line of scrimmage. No player may be blocked below the waist after he goes beyond the line. It is illegal for a player to jump on, stand on, lean on, or be picked up by a teammate to gain additional height to block a kick.

Penalties: illegal blocking on kicks, or illegal attempt to block the kick, 15 yards.

Fair Catch. A member of the receiving team may signal his intention to make a fair catch of any free kick or kick from scrimmage, by raising an arm one full length above his head while the kick is in flight. Once he has signaled for a fair catch, no opponent may interfere with him, the ball, or his path to the ball.

The player who signals for the fair catch does not have to catch the ball, but he then may not make contact with a member of the kicking team until the ball touches a player. If he catches the ball, he may not advance it. If the ball hits the ground or is touched by a member of the kicking team, the fair-catch signal is off and all the rules for a kicked ball apply.

After a fair catch is made, the receiving team may elect to put the ball

in play by a snap from the mark of the catch or by a free kick. If time expires while the ball is in play, and a fair catch is awarded, the receiving team may choose to extend the period with one free kick.

Penalties: invalid fair-catch signal, receivers' ball 5 yards behind the spot of invalid signal; fair-catch interference, 15 yards from spot of foul and catch awarded.

Enforcement of Kicking Penalties. Fouls during a free kick or kick from scrimmage are enforced from the previous spot or line of scrimmage, except that penalties for interference with a fair catch or an invalid fair-catch signal are enforced from the spot of the foul.

If, on a scrimmage kick, the receiving team commits a foul while the ball is in the air or on the ground, before gaining possession, the receiving team retains possession but is penalized for its foul.

If a kick is simultaneously recovered by two opposing players, possession is awarded to the receiving team.

PENALTY REFUSED — **UNSPORTSMANLIKE CONDUCT** OR **FOULS DISREGARDED** — **PLAYER DISQUALIFIED**

■ ENFORCEMENT OF PENALTIES

Spot of Enforcement. A penalty for a foul can be enforced from one of four basic spots: (1) the spot where the foul was committed, (2) the spot where the act connected with the foul (such as a snap, pass, fumble, or kick) occurred, (3) the previous spot where the ball was put in play, (4) the succeeding spot where the ball would next be put in play if no penalty were enforced.

Spots of enforcement with regard to particular penalties have been listed in the preceding sections. The following rules take precedence, however:

All fouls committed by the offense behind the line of scrimmage, fouls by the offense beyond the line of scrimmage when the runner is downed behind the line of scrimmage, and fouls by the defense for illegal use of hands, arms, or body behind the line of scrimmage, are penalized from the previous spot.

Except as above, when the offense commits a foul behind the normal spot of enforcement, the spot of enforcement is the spot of the foul.

When a foul occurs on a running play, the spot of enforcement is the spot where the ball is dead (unless the preceding rules apply).

If the spot of enforcement has not been specified or is not governed by the above rules, it is the spot of the foul. (As complicated as the above may seem, there are many more exceptions and special situations governing the spot of enforcement that are not mentioned here.)

Down Number. When the offense is penalized for a foul for which there is a distance penalty only (not combined with a loss-of-down penalty), the down number of the next play remains the same as for the play in which the foul occurred.

After a penalty for a foul by the defense, the next down is first and ten for the offense, except that with regard to offside and encroachment, excess time outs and delay of game, or illegal substitution by the defense, the down number and first-down line (for necessary yardage) remain the same for the offense.

Distance of Penalty. If the enforcement of a distance penalty would place the ball more than half the distance to the offender's goal line, the penalty is half the distance to its goal line.

The defense, when near its goal line, may not deliberately commit continued fouls to prevent a score.

Penalty: fouls to prevent a score, score awarded (if violation is repeated after warning).

Refusal of Penalties. Penalties for all fouls may be declined by the captain of the offended team, in which case play proceeds as though the foul had not been committed.

Multiple and Double Fouls. If the same team commits two fouls during the same down ('multiple' foul), only one penalty may be enforced. The captain of the offended team must make the choice after the referee has explained the alternatives.

If both teams commit fouls during the same down ('double' foul) and possession of the ball does not change, the penalties are offset and the down is replayed at the previous spot, except that if one of the fouls incurs a 15-yard penalty and the other a 5-yard penalty, the major penalty yardage is assessed from the previous spot.

If there is a double foul during which there is a change of possession (as on a kicking play, fumble, or intercepted pass), the team last gaining possession may keep the ball after enforcement for its foul, unless its foul was committed prior to the change of possession, in which case the penalties are offset as described in the paragraph above. If a double foul occurs after a change of possession, the team in possession may retain possession at the spot its foul occurred, but not in advance of the dead ball spot.

If, during a kickoff or punt, the kicking team fouls before possession changes and the receiving team fouls after possession changes, the penalties are offset and the down is replayed.

Fouls During or After Scoring. If a foul is committed by the defense during a down in which there is a score by touchdown, field goal, extra point, or safety (or after a touchdown and before the whistle for the extra-point try), the penalty is assessed on the following kickoff.

Addressing Officials. No player other than the team's captain may address an official about a rule interpretation or attempt to exercise a captain's privileges, except in an emergency.

Penalty: illegally addressing official, 5 yards from succeeding spot.

Unsportsmanlike Conduct. Unsportsmanlike conduct is any act that is contrary to the generally understood principles of sportsmanship, including using abusive language to players or officials or taunting or baiting acts, using substitutes to confuse players or to conserve or consume time, attempting to disconcert the offensive team at the snap, concealing the ball underneath clothing, and throwing a punch, forearm, or kick even though no contact is made.

Penalty: unsportsmanlike conduct, 15 yards from succeeding spot (if ball is dead) or previous spot (if ball is in play), plus disqualification if flagrant.

Disqualification. A player may be banished from further participation in the game for flagrant instances of striking an opponent, roughing the passer or kicker, unsportsmanlike conduct, and for palpably unfair acts. A disqualified player must return to his dressing room and may not reappear in his team uniform or return to any area except those to which spectators have access.

Penalties: palpably unfair act, disqualification and distance penalty as deemed equitable; return of disqualified player, 15 yards and exclusion of player from playing enclosure.

■ THE OFFICIALS AND THEIR DUTIES

The Referee. The referee is the top official on the field. He has overall control of the game and is the final judge if there is any disagreement over rules or infractions of rules. He positions himself in the offensive backfield about ten yards behind the line of scrimmage, on the right side of the field (if the quarterback is right-handed).

The referee's first job is to watch the offensive backfield men to make sure their motion is legal and to watch the snap to make sure it is legally executed.

On a running play, the referee first watches the quarterback until he has handed off the ball and the play has proceeded down the field. Once the quarterback is clear of defenders, the referee follows the play, watching the ball carrier and making sure there is not any illegal contact behind the play. Once the ball carrier has been tackled, the referee checks with the official nearest the tackle to see where the runner's forward progress was stopped and spots the ball for the next play.

On a passing play, the referee drops back with the quarterback while checking to see that the blocking of the linemen is legal. As the defenders get closer to the quarterback, the referee concentrates his attention completely on the quarterback to make sure he is not roughed by a defensive man after having thrown the pass. The referee is also responsible for determining whether to call a fumble or incomplete pass if the ball comes loose while the quarterback is passing or preparing to pass.

On a kicking play, the job of the referee is to watch the kicker and make sure he is not illegally hit by a man on the defensive team.

After a foul, the referee must announce the penalty to both captains and explain the options to the offended team's captain. After enforcement, the referee signals the nature of the penalty to the spectators. The referee also must notify the coach when a team has used its three time outs, when two minutes remain in the half, and when a player has been disqualified.

The Umpire. The primary area of responsibility of the umpire is the line of scrimmage. He positions himself on the defensive side of the field, about five yards from the line of scrimmage and either a little to the right or to the left of the football.

The umpire first looks for a false start by the offensive linemen. Once the ball has been snapped, he watches both the offensive and defensive linemen to make sure their blocking activity is legal.

On a passing play, the umpire immediately moves up to the line of scrimmage so that he can judge whether any offensive linemen move illegally downfield. If the play turns into a screen pass, he moves so that he can watch the intended receiver and the blocking activity involving him. The umpire also helps judge whether a pass is complete or incomplete in his area of the playing field.

Finally, the umpire is in charge of ruling on the legality of the players' equipment.

The Head Linesman. The head linesman takes a position on one of the sidelines, at the line of scrimmage. His first job is to look for encroachment, offside, and false starts at the line of scrimmage prior to the snap.

On a pass play, the head linesman makes sure that pass receivers on his side of the field are not illegally hit within five yards of the line of scrimmage. He is responsible for calling pass interference in his area.

The head linesman is responsible for determining if a runner or pass receiver goes out of bounds on his side of the field and also helps determine the forward progress of the ball carrier. In general, he is responsible for determining and calling any infraction in his area of the field whether the play involves a run, pass, or kick.

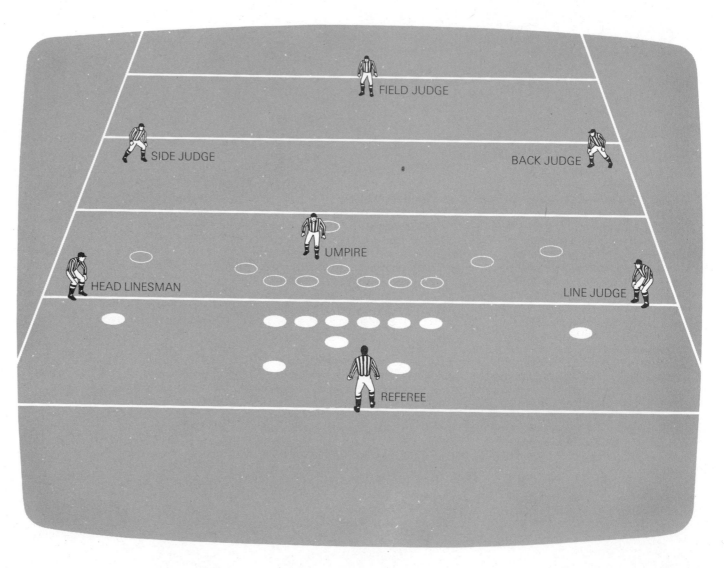

FIELD JUDGE

SIDE JUDGE

BACK JUDGE

UMPIRE

HEAD LINESMAN

LINE JUDGE

REFEREE

Finally, the head linesman helps the referee keep track of the down numbers. He is also responsible for the chain crew and assists them in bringing the chain out on the field to measure for a first down.

The Line Judge. On the opposite side of the field from the head linesman is the line judge, who stands with one foot on each side of the line of scrimmage.

The line judge's first job is to watch for any offside activity prior to the start of the play. Then he makes sure that the wide receiver on his side of the field is not illegally hit . Once the receiver has cleared this area, the line judge moves to the offensive backfield. He must rule whether any pass is a forward or backward pass and whether a pass has been thrown before or after the passer crosses the line of scrimmage. In general, the line judge observes and rules on all activity in his area of the field.

On a punt, the line judge stays on the line of scrimmage to make sure that only the two end offensive players move downfield before the ball is kicked. He judges whether the kick has crossed the line of scrimmage and then follows the kicking unit downfield as they cover the punt.

The line judge also is responsible for keeping track of the time of the game. He carries a stopwatch as a backup for the stadium clock operator.

The Back Judge. The back judge is on the same side of the field as the line judge. He operates in an area about seventeen yards downfield from the line of scrimmage and is primarily responsible for all rulings in this area involving the sideline.

The back judge concentrates on the end or running back on his side of the field. He rules on all offensive and defensive infractions either by or against these players. The back judge also rules on catches, recovery of fumbles, and illegal touching of the football beyond the line of scrimmage. He calls pass interference, blocking, and tackling infractions that occur in his area and looks for potential clipping penalties on punt returns.

Finally, along with the field judge, the back judge rules on whether a field goal try is successful or not.

The Side Judge. Also seventeen yards downfield, opposite the back judge and on the same side of the field as the head linesman, is the side judge. His responsibilities on his side of the field are the same as those of the back judge.

The Field Judge. The field judge stations himself about twenty-five yards downfield, approximately in line with the tight end. He follows the activity of the tight end and those who defend against him. He also watches the ends and backs and rules on any activity involving them in his deep area. In general, he is responsible for calling all infractions from his position whether the play is a run, pass, or kick.

The field judge is responsible for keeping the 30-second clock. He also times the intervals between the quarters.

Responsibilities of Officials.

All the officials have jurisdiction over any foul committed in the game; there is no territorial division of responsibilities for calling fouls. When an official sees a foul committed, he reports it to the referee, informing him of its nature, the position of the ball at the time of the foul, the offender, and the spot of enforcement of the foul.

All the officials are also responsible of a rule, its interpretation, or its enforcement. If an official makes an error in the interpretation of a rule, the other officials must check him before play is resumed; otherwise, they are equally responsible. In the event of a disagreement, the crew should confer. If the officials' vote is tied, the referee's vote is the deciding factor.

■ COLLEGE FOOTBALL RULES

The rules for college football differ slightly from those of the professional National Football League. Some of the most important differences are summarized below.

The hash marks on the field are only 53 feet, 4 inches in from the sidelines.

The offensive team has only twenty-five seconds between plays to huddle and put the ball back in play.

On the try for additional score after a touchdown, the team is awarded one point for kicking the ball through the goal post uprights and two points if it runs or passes the ball across the goal line.

A pass reception is complete if the receiver has one foot in bounds when he has possession of the ball.

Pass blocking must be with the elbows outside the blocker's frame and hands inside. Fists may not be used. Blocking below the waist is forbidden on pass interceptions (as well as on kicking plays).

The kickoff is from the kicking team's 40-yard line.

■ CANADIAN FOOTBALL RULES

There are major differences between the rules for professional football in the United States and those of the Canadian Football League. This section highlights some of the most interesting and significant variances.

The field is 110 yards long and 65 yards wide, with 20-yard end zones.

Each team plays with twelve men on the field. The extra offensive backfield man usually plays in a wing position. The defense has two 'defensive halfbacks' in place of the strong safety.

There are no time outs, except at the two-minute warnings.

If a kick is not returned out of the end zone, the kicking team is awarded one point, called a 'single'.

The offense must gain ten yards in three downs or relinquish the ball to the opposition. (This rule forces the offense to favor a passing attack.)

Because of the extra offensive back, there are seven eligible receivers (including the quarterback). All offensive backs can be in motion prior to the play and can move in any direction, including toward the line of scrimmage.

The defense may line up no closer than one yard from the football. (This rule, along with the offensive motion rule, makes it relatively easy to run for short yardage.)

When a ball carrier is knocked down he must be held down. If a fumble goes out of bounds, possession is awarded to the team that last touched the ball. A fumble may be batted or kicked in any direction.

On a punt, the punter and any member of the punting team who was behind the punter when the ball was kicked may recover the ball for the punting team. Furthermore, the punter may not be blocked. (These rules allow the punter to short kick and not face blockers or tacklers in his attempt to recover the ball.)

There is no fair-catch rule, but members of the kicking team must stay at least five yards from the return man until he catches or touches the football.

Each team is allowed only thirty-two players on its roster. (This rule, along with the twelve-man team, forces players to play more than one position, including special teams assignments.)

Canadian teams often are scheduled to play more than once a week and as often as four times in twelve days. Some teams play on Friday evening and again on Sunday afternoon.

Index of
Football Terms